# best practices

# for faculty

# search

# committees

**Other Books** by Jeffrey L. Buller

# best practices

# for faculty

# search

# committees

how to review applications
and interview candidates

jeffrey l. buller

**JB JOSSEY-BASS**™
A Wiley Brand

Published by Jossey-Bass
A Wiley Brand
One Montgomery Street, Suite 1000, San Francisco, CA 94104-4594—www.josseybass.com

Jossey-Bass books and products are available through most bookstores. To contact Jossey-Bass directly call our Customer Care Department within the U.S. at 800-956-7739, outside the U.S. at 317-572-3986, or fax 317-572-4002.

Wiley publishes in a variety of print and electronic formats and by print-on-demand. Some material included with standard print versions of this book may not be included in e-books or in print-on-demand. If this book refers to media such as a CD or DVD that is not included in the version you purchased, you may download this material at http://booksupport.wiley.com. For more information about Wiley products, visit www.wiley.com.

**Library of Congress Cataloging-in-Publication Data**

Names: Buller, Jeffrey L., author.
Title: Best practices for faculty search committees: how to review applications
    and interview candidates / Jeffrey L. Buller.
Description: San Francisco, CA : Jossey-Bass ; Hoboken, NJ : John Wiley &
    Sons, 2017. | Includes bibliographical references and index.
Identifiers: LCCN 2016038235 (print) | LCCN 2016050844 (ebook) | ISBN
    9781119349969 (cloth : alk. paper) | ISBN 9781119351665 (Adobe PDF) | ISBN
    9781119351658 (ePub)
Subjects: LCSH: Universities and colleges—Faculty—Employment. | Employment
    interviewing. | Employee selection.
Classification: LCC LB2332.7 .B85 2017 (print) | LCC LB2332.7 (ebook) | DDC
    378.1/2—dc23
LC record available at https://lccn.loc.gov/2016038235

Cover design: Wiley

Printed in the United States of America
FIRST EDITION
*HB Printing*   10  9  8  7  6  5  4  3  2  1

*For Robert E. Cipriano ("Collegial Bob") without whom ATLAS Leadership Training would not exist and my life would be immeasurably diminished.*

# contents

# the author

Jeffrey L. Buller has served in administrative positions ranging from department chair to vice president for academic affairs at four very different institutions: Loras College, Georgia Southern University, Mary Baldwin College, and Florida Atlantic University. He is the author of 13 books on higher education administration, a textbook for first-year college students, and a book of essays on the music dramas of Richard Wagner. Buller has also written numerous articles on Greek and Latin literature, 19th- and 20th-century opera, and college administration. From 2003 to 2005, he served as the principal English language lecturer at the International Wagner Festival in Bayreuth, Germany. More recently, he has been active as a consultant to the Ministry of Education in Saudi Arabia, where he is assisting with the creation of a kingdom-wide academic leadership center. Along with Robert E. Cipriano, Buller is a senior partner in ATLAS: Academic Training, Leadership, & Assessment Services, through which he has presented numerous workshops on academic leadership and faculty searches.

# introduction

For many faculty members, serving on a search committee is one of those activities that they think they ought to understand—after all, when they themselves were applicants, they did well enough with at least one search committee to be offered a job—but that becomes more and more puzzling the further they become involved in the process. Why do institutions have all these cumbersome procedures they have to follow? How can the search committee deal with reading all the applications that come in and still have time for its members to do their teaching and research? What questions do you ask in an interview to find out the things that you really want to know? What questions *shouldn't* you ask, and how much trouble will you be in if you do? Although there are a few resources available on the technical aspects of how to run a search, a search committee will find very little available to review quickly so that they can get their task done properly and efficiently. As a result, faculty searches can be hit or miss. Sometimes everything seems to fall into place, and the search committee ends up hiring a wonderful new faculty member who becomes not only an important colleague but also a person who brings new vitality to the discipline. At other times, the applicant who seemed so perfect on paper and during the interview ends up being a very different type of person once the hiring process is complete, and the program as a whole suffers as a result.

This brief guidebook is intended to help make faculty search committees more effective and to make the work of serving on one if not easy then at least a little easier than it otherwise might have been. I wrote this book with busy college professors in mind, keeping what they need to know clear, concise, and above all practical. You're probably not reading this book to gain a theoretical overview of how faculty searches potentially could be run. You're probably reading it because you're involved in a search *now* and you want to know what to do. For that reason, I've structured *Best Practices for Faculty Search Committees* so that it can be used in three different ways:

- You can read it straight through from beginning to end and gain a solid understanding of what you need to do as a member of a faculty search committee.
- You can jump immediately to whichever chapter contains a topic on some aspect of faculty searches that you need.
- You can browse through it casually and pick up a few pointers or best practices along the way.

In fact, to make the casual use of the book more productive, I've formatted the text at certain points to highlight the most important concepts for readers to return to and for casual browsers to find more easily.

> Passages in boxes such as this are concise summaries of the best practices referred to in the book's title. They've been set apart so that they'll be easy for you to find again when you've finished reading this book or for others to find when they're just flipping through the pages.

I'd like to express my gratitude to Magna Publications for granting me permission to reprint material from "What Every Search Committee Will Tell You," *Academic Leader* (March 2014) 30(3), 4–5 in Chapter 3 and "Searches With Incumbents or Internal Candidates," *Academic Leader* (May 2009) 25(5), 4–5 in Chapter 4. I'd also like to thank Sandy Ogden for editorial advice and Selene Vazquez for research assistance. They both played a significant role in making this book better than it otherwise would have been.

Serving on a search committee can be difficult work, requiring long hours and elaborate attention to details. But the end result—a new colleague who can help our programs and institutions improve and possibly become an important part of our own professional growth—makes all that effort worthwhile. I wish you nothing but the best in your own searches, and I hope to hear of your successes in putting these ideas into practice. You can reach me at jbuller@atlasleadership.com or through our website www.atlasleadership.com.

# 1

# achieving diversity goals

Since about 1980, one of the most commonly repeated themes during the faculty interview process is the need to make sure that a finalist pool is sufficiently diverse. At times, this emphasis on diversity assumes a level of importance that nearly equals the attention given to the credentials and experience of the applicants. To be sure, higher education's intense focus on diversity sometimes seems unusual to people who work outside of academia. "Sure, we all want to follow policies that aren't discriminatory when we build a workforce," someone might say, "but diversity almost seems like an obsession to college professors today. Why can't you just decide to hire the best applicant regardless of race, gender, country of origin, or any other factor that's irrelevant to the requirements of the job?" But hiring the best applicant is precisely what higher education's diversity goals are all about. So, as an initial step in increasing the diversity of an applicant pool, let's begin by reminding ourselves why this goal is important to us in the first place.

The first reason why a diverse faculty (as well as a diverse staff, administration, and student body) is important at colleges and universities is to *correct past injustices*. For many years in American higher education, the vast majority of the professoriate consisted of White males of European ancestry. People who didn't fit that profile were discouraged—sometimes blatantly, sometimes subtly—from pursuing an academic career. Moreover, for most of their history, a significant number of institutions enrolled only a single gender, with the result that men's colleges and universities had an almost exclusively male faculty, and even most women's colleges and universities had a faculty that consisted mostly of men. The existence of historically Black colleges and universities meant that some schools only admitted White students, whereas Black students were often encouraged to attend the historically Black institutions, even when all universities were technically open to them. The result was that most institutions had a faculty that was almost exclusively White, and historically Black institutions had a faculty that was almost exclusively Black. Following the ruling of the US Supreme Court in 1954 in the case of *Brown v. Board of Education*, it was increasingly recognized by professional educators that the doctrine of "separate but equal" wasn't working at *any* level of education. Most universities became more integrated racially throughout the 1960s, and then, in the early 1970s, a large number of men's colleges began admitting women.

Those historical injustices may seem like ancient history now, but they've had a lasting effect. In 2014, 77.4% of the US population was White, 13.2% was Black, 17.4% regarded themselves as Hispanic or Latino, and 50.8% were women (U.S. Census Bureau, n.d.). As the National Center for Education Statistics has reported,

> In fall 2013, of all full-time faculty in degree-granting postsecondary institutions, 79 percent were White (43 percent were White males and 35 percent were White females), 6 percent were Black, 5 percent were Hispanic, and 10 percent were Asian/Pacific Islander .... The percentage of all faculty who were female increased from 39 percent in 1993 to 49 percent in 2013. (National Center for Education Statistics, n.d.)

So, although there's been progress in promoting the representation of women on the faculty, the percentage of Blacks and Hispanics still lags significantly behind their representation in the population overall. These matters are of concern at colleges and universities because institutions of higher education view themselves as sources of opportunity and positive social change. If even the people who are most vocal about providing fair representation in employment are not achieving their own goals, what hope can there be for the rest of society to do so? As a result, members of search committees often feel that they're under a moral obligation to make the faculty more diverse than it already is.

The second reason for considering matters of diversity when building faculty positions and conducting searches is that it *adds significant pedagogical value* to a program. The world in which graduates of our institutions will live and work is highly diverse. They must feel comfortable working alongside people who look at the world very differently from how they themselves view matters, come from very different social and economic backgrounds, and want very different things from their lives. Students become more adept at negotiating their way through a diverse world by being exposed to a diverse educational environment from prekindergarten through graduate school. Moreover, a diverse faculty is likely to challenge students' thinking in ways that a more homogeneous faculty won't. By reflecting on their basic assumptions about how projects that benefit humanity are selected for funding, how to find balance and meaning in their own lives, and how best to provide for their families without promoting inequity for other people's families, students gain in critical thinking skills, learn to defend their values more effectively, and understand when it becomes necessary and acceptable simply to agree to disagree with others.

Because providing a diverse intellectual and social environment for students is so important in higher education, is it also important to add positions and conduct searches in such a way as to attain a faculty that's diverse in terms of its political views? Certainly, the criticism is often made that the US professoriate is far more liberal than society at large. Books such as Roger Kimball's *Tenured Radicals* (2008) and Ben Shapiro's *Brainwashed* (2004), along with films such as Evan Coyne Maloney's *Indoctrinate U* (Maloney, E. C., & On the Fence Films, 2004), argue that liberal elites at colleges and universities perpetuate themselves by teaching students to think exactly like them and only hiring other professors who share their beliefs. Isn't it hypocritical of the academy, therefore, to claim that it's committed to diversity when it comes to race and gender but not when it comes to ideology, the very area that an institution supposedly devoted to advanced learning should care most about? Shouldn't we be pursuing political diversity as well?

Certainly, search committees should be cognizant of these issues as they design their positions and plan their searches. But it's also important to understand the context in which certain claims and counterclaims are being made. A number of surveys do suggest that the US professoriate is more liberal than the public at large (see, for example, Hurtado, Eagan, Pryor, Whang, & Tran, 2012; Jaschik, 2012; and Kurtz, 2005). But there are several important factors that skew these data:

- The population that chooses to attend a college or university identifies itself as more liberal than the population that chooses other paths in life (see Jennings & Stoker, 2008). Because a college faculty is, by necessity, a subset of those who attended a college or university, it is all but inevitable that college professors will be more liberal than the population at large.
- Because college professors belong to a public service segment of the economy in which salaries are traditionally lower than in the corporate world, more liberals (who value advancing the good of society over personal gain) than conservatives (who value personal freedom and success over social welfare projects) tend to be attracted to academic life.
- Neil Gross (2013) argues in *Why Are Professors Liberal and Why Do Conservatives Care?* that American conservatism in the post–William Buckley age has frequently defined itself in terms of its opposition to liberal intellectual elites. As such, we shouldn't expect many neoconservatives to be seeking employment in the academy because that would be tantamount to joining forces with "the enemy."

Moreover, despite the fact that professors tend to be more liberal than the population at large, if their goal is to indoctrinate the youth, they've proven themselves to be singularly bad at it. In study performed by Mack Mariani of Xavier University and Gordon J. Hewitt of Hamilton College (2008), it was discovered that the shift toward liberalism that occurs among traditional-aged college students is no greater than that which occurs in general among the population aged 18 to 24. Does all this information mean that search committees can be blithely indifferent to the question of ideological diversity on the faculty? Absolutely not. Students should—and, I would argue, *do*—receive exposure to a full range of political perspectives during their college careers. But it's just as unreasonable to expect that the percentage of conservatives on a college faculty will reflect that of the general population as it is to expect that the percentage of creationists in a biology department will reflect that of the general population. There may be a larger pool of conservative humanists than there are creationist biologists, but the same factors we previously outlined make that pool fairly small in any case. Our goal, therefore, should be to avoid *excluding* a qualified candidate from our finalist pool simply because he or she differs from us in political ideology rather than to try to construct some sort of affirmative action program for conservatives (who would probably be philosophically opposed to that idea anyway).

The third reason why diversity needs to be considered in matters of faculty recruitment is that it *provides students with a broader range of role models*. No one would deny that all good college professors want to serve as positive role models for all their students and that many students have role models who differ from them in race, ethnicity, gender, and other ways. In fact, one strength of a highly diverse educational environment is that students *do* begin to see people who are very different from them as mentors and examples to emulate. Nevertheless, it does send an unintended message that a certain field or profession doesn't really welcome people of certain backgrounds if students never see a member of their own race, ethnicity, or gender working in those positions. For this reason, colleges and universities often make diversity one of their goals in faculty searches as a way of encouraging the broadest possible range of students to consider various options for careers, fields of study, and ways of life.

## ○  affirmative action and equal opportunity

One of the most common misunderstandings in faculty searches is how the concepts of affirmative action and equal opportunity relate to an institution's diversity goals. The first area of misunderstanding arises from the assumption that affirmative action and equal opportunity are the same thing. They're not. Providing equal opportunity relates to what institutions *shouldn't be doing* in its searches; affirmative action relates to what they *should be doing*. In other words, although equal opportunity offers *passive protection* ("We consider everyone equally, no matter who they are."), affirmative action strives for *active inclusion* ("We take steps to make sure our applicant pools are suitably diverse."). Providing equal opportunity means that applicants for a position won't be discriminated against because of factors such as race, gender, ethnicity, sexual orientation, and the like. Participating in affirmative action means that an institution is making a conscious and systematic effort to undo the lingering effects of past discrimination, ensure that all applicants have an equal opportunity to be considered for a position, and base its hiring decisions only on valid, job-related criteria.

Affirmative action is thus a more highly structured process than simply offering equal opportunity to all candidates for employment consideration. In the United States, affirmative action began as a series of executive orders under presidents Kennedy and Johnson that required government agencies and other entities holding federal contracts to be systematic in giving due consideration for employment to members of various groups who had previously faced discrimination. The groups included in affirmative action policies evolved over time, eventually addressing issues of race, gender, creed, color, and national origin. Different laws protect other groups that are not explicitly addressed under federal affirmative action laws, such as veterans, people with physical challenges, and those over 40 years of age. Some of these laws similarly require employers who accept federal contracts—at times, the laws specify that this regulation applies only when the federal contracts are of a certain minimum size and when the hiring institution has a certain minimum number of employees—to engage in systematic efforts to hire people from these additional protected groups. As public institutions, colleges and universities are generally viewed as venues where affirmative action must be applied. But technically speaking, unless an institution accepts federal contracts, it's not *required* to engage in affirmative action, even though it may choose to do so for other reasons. For this reason, the notion that all institutions of higher education are required to have affirmative action plans in place constitutes the second major misunderstanding about affirmative action and equal opportunity.

The third misunderstanding occurs when people believe that the expression *protected class* means something it doesn't. In higher education, this expression can be used in three (not always synonymous) ways. First, there are *federal protected classes*. These are the groups who are protected from discrimination by laws that apply everywhere in the United States. By chronological order in which these laws were enacted, it is against federal law in the United States to discriminate against anyone for the following reasons:

- Race
- Skin color
- Religion
- National origin
- Sex
- Pregnancy status
- Family status
- Disability status

In addition, for employment purposes, it is illegal to discriminate against people because they belong to one of the following groups:

- Veterans
- People over the age of 40
- Citizens of other countries, provided that they are legally eligible to work in the United States
- Predisposed to any illness or health condition because of genetic factors

The second category of protected classes consists of *state-designated protected classes*. For example, in the state of Maryland, protected class status is extended to matters of sexual orientation and gender identity (State of Maryland Commission on Civil Rights, n.d.). In California, this classification includes matters of an applicant's AIDS/HIV status, political activities or affiliations, and status as a victim of domestic violence, assault, or stalking. Because states vary somewhat in the groups included in their categories of protected classes, it's a good practice for search committees—particularly if they include members who have relocated from other states—to become familiar with all state statutes on discrimination that apply to a search.

The third category of protected classes are those mentioned in an *institution's nondiscrimination statement*. It's not usual for colleges and universities to provide protection that extends far beyond what state and federal laws require. For example, they may provide protection not merely on the basis of gender identity (which could be a matter of state law) but also gender expression, transition status from one gender to another, transgender status, and gender nonconformity. Complicating this entire issue is that private institutions may be exempt from certain of these policies if an issue relates directly to their mission and identity. In this way, an evangelical Christian college could give priority to or even require applicants to be evangelical Christians. A women's college might give preference to applicants for faculty, staff, and administrative positions if the applicants are women. So, even though people in searches will often speak of the need to take "protected classes" into account when the search is being conducted, they may not be aware of which classes are truly protected in that search. Particularly in the case of institution-specific versus federal- or state-mandated protected classes in employment, the problems that can be caused by failing to follow a requirement could vary considerably. After all, it's one thing to receive a stern reprimand from the institution's president and another thing entirely to discover that you may be liable to stiff fines and imprisonment.

## ○ the problem with unnecessary specialization

Given that colleges and universities are required to avoid discrimination in hiring and usually are quite eager to diversify their faculty, what are some effective ways of achieving these goals? Some institutions think it's enough to include in their advertisements a line such as "Women and minorities encouraged to apply." or "An affirmative action/equal employment opportunity institution." Although better than nothing, those efforts are unlikely to get the schools very far in their efforts to diversify their applicant pools. Successful diversity efforts begin with the design of the position itself, not the phrasing of the advertisement. Here are a few factors to make sure that your chair and dean are aware of as they approve how faculty vacancies are defined:

- Although for the purposes of accreditation and the preservation of academic quality it's important for faculty members to be properly credentialed, academic positions are sometimes developed in such a way that their required qualifications restrict them unnecessarily. For example, many advertisements describe a position as requiring a PhD when other kinds of doctorates (such as a DA, PsyD, or EdD) or other terminal degrees (such as an MFA or MLS) would also be appropriate credentials for someone in that discipline. Although some institutions will be flexible enough to let a search committee hire a candidate with an EdD when a PhD was cited as a requirement in search advertisements, others won't. Moreover, a highly desirable candidate with a different type of terminal degree may not even apply for the position when he or she sees the words *PhD required* in the advertisement. Because developing a diverse applicant pool is easier when you put fewer unnecessary hurdles in a candidate's way, list as requirements only what would be *absolutely essential* in order to perform the duties of the position. Using the standards set by your accrediting body or including the words "terminal degree in a field closely related to the discipline" is often preferable to limiting your applicants to only those who have earned PhDs.

- Consider how narrowly the academic field of the candidate truly has to be in order to achieve your area's goals for this position. Suppose that Overly Specialized State University created a position for an economist who specialized in medieval and Renaissance Flemish prenuptial agreements. Would that program truly not be interested in an economist who brought the area greater diversity but who didn't specialized in Renaissance and early modern Flemish prenuptial agreements? Sometimes certain restrictions are necessary: The program absolutely could not teach its curriculum or meet its research obligations unless it hires a faculty member with a very specific set of credentials. But in most cases, the narrow focus of a position stems from the preferences of people in the program, not genuine needs or curricular requirements. Just as it's easier to broaden the diversity of a candidate pool if we broaden the type of academic credentials we seek in a search, so is it easier to expand the pool if we expand a position's academic focus as much as possible while still meeting the program's legitimate needs.
- At other times, we can create diversity in our programs by creating positions in specialties that traditionally have attracted a diverse group of graduate students. Although it's wrong to assume that women are interested in a field only if it's approached from a women's studies perspective or that African Americans are interested in a field only if it's approached from an African American studies perspective, the fact is that the majority of graduate students in most women's studies programs are women and the majority of graduate students in most African American studies programs are Black. So, if it makes sense to do so in your discipline, you can increase the likelihood of attracting a diverse applicant pool by designing positions to include specialties that traditionally attract a diverse group of graduate students.

## ○ support from institutional leadership

Another major factor that can affect the success of a diversity plan is the extent of support the plan receives from the institution's administration. If the president and provost seem indifferent to the notion that faculty diversity is important—or even if they only give these issues lip service unaccompanied by any concrete action—department chairs and members of search committees are unlikely to regard this topic as a high priority. It can be very useful, therefore, for the school's administration to discuss the contribution that diversity makes to the institution, not merely occasionally (such as when charging a search committee) but repeatedly, whenever there is occasion to talk about the institution's future direction. The concrete actions that the administration can take in advancing the school's diversity goals include the following:

- Funding travel by the search chair or members of the committee to conferences in the discipline that are known to attract diverse audiences. Posting job notices, prescreening possible candidates, and talking about the position with conference attendees can all result in a far more diverse pool than otherwise might be obtained.
- Providing support to successful applicants who add significantly to the institution's diversity. This type of support could take many different forms. For instance, a college or university may be seeking a candidate with a terminal degree but find an otherwise highly qualified candidate from a minority group or protected class who has not yet completed his or her dissertation. The upper administration could authorize the hiring of the candidate, with a research budget but highly reduced workload, until the candidate's terminal degree is granted. The promotion and tenure clock might be stopped temporarily to enable the candidate time to complete his or her dissertation. And assistance might be provided to find employment for a spouse or life partner so as to make the candidate's relocation easier.
- If the faculty member who is hired will be joining a very small community of others who share his or her gender, ethnicity, sexual orientation, and the like, administrators can be proactive in establishing support groups and contacts within the community who can help the newcomer feel more at home at the institution and less isolated by his or her minority status.

Administrators also make a contribution toward an institution's diversity goals when they help enact policies that require search committees to pay attention to issues of diversity. The most common way of enforcing this requirement is to mandate that all lists of semifinalists and finalists be approved before phone interviews are conducted or invitations to campus interviews are issued. The role of the administration in diversifying the faculty thus has critical symbolic and practical elements throughout the search process. Administrators serve as the face of the institution to internal and external stakeholders, actively shape the policies and procedures that the institution uses to conduct its business, and interpret federal and state requirements to all the institution's stakeholders. As a result, it's all but impossible for a school to achieve its goals of faculty diversity if the administration isn't fully engaged in and committed to the importance of that goal.

## o  composition of the search committee

Another important strategy for attaining your institution's leadership goals can best be achieved by balancing the composition of the search committee. In many cases, when people first learn about this strategy, they think, "The goal here must be to make sure that every search committee includes representation from minority groups and protected classes." Certainly, including this type of representation brings a number of benefits. It increases the likelihood that highly qualified candidates from minority groups or protected classes won't inadvertently be overlooked, sends a message to the candidates being interviewed that the institution values diversity, and provides minority candidates someone to speak with on the committee who is likely to understand their issues and concerns. But there's also a downside to this approach: Because minority faculty members are, by definition, fewer in number than those in the majority, the same faculty members end up serving on committee after committee, sometimes to the detriment of their teaching and research. Black and Latino faculty members (as well as women in fields where they are traditionally underrepresented) often feel that their service load is exceptionally high, with every committee, task force, and council at the institution needing a minority representative. There is even a term for this type of over-assignment of minorities to committees for the purposes of representation and diversity: *cultural taxation* (see June, 2015). And it's a phenomenon that most members of minority groups on college faculties experience regularly.

How then can you structure the composition of the search committee in such a way that it increases the likelihood of receiving applications from a large enough pool of highly qualified minority candidates without becoming a burden on the minority faculty members already at the institution? One solution that many schools have found useful is to appoint at least one member of each search committee to serve as the group's *diversity advocate*, regardless of whether he or she is a member of any minority group or protected class. For example, the search procedures of George Washington University (GWU) state that every member of the search committee is responsible for helping the institution reach its goals for diversity, but the specially designated diversity advocate on each search committee has special responsibilities with regard to this role. At GWU, the diversity advocate is expected to do the following:

- Be a vocal and responsible advocate for diversity and inclusion keeping in mind the goals and principles of diversity [that the institution has developed].
- Actively monitor each stage of the search process to ensure an equitable and open search that is consistent with the goals established at the outset of the process.
- Facilitate thoughtful exchanges about how diversity can help the department close the gap between the current state and aspirations (e.g., attract a broader mix of majors or graduate students, mentor diverse students, offer different curricular or research opportunities, attract funding, and so forth).
- Lead discussions related to strategies for developing a diverse pool that could lead to attracting and hiring women, persons of color, persons with disabilities, and veterans. Keep the issues at

the center of every strategic conversation and each phase of the decision-making process.

- Assist the committee in self-scrutiny about potential biases towards, for example, identity group or academic affiliations. Encourage search committee members to think about how innate schemas may lead to unconscious and unintended bias in how members relate to individuals/events/information throughout the evaluation and selection process. (The George Washington University, n.d.)

Similarly, the University of Illinois at Urbana-Champaign defines a diversity advocate as the following:

an individual designated on the search form by the department executive officer [at the] time the search is initiated. The individual should be committed to being an advocate for diversity as a core component of diversity in the search process. For tenure and tenure-track faculty searches, the Diversity Advocate must be a tenured faculty member. For academic professional positions, the Diversity Advocate must be a member of the search committee. (Office of Diversity, Equity, and Access, 2015)

As this description makes clear, it's more important for a diversity advocate to be *committed* to the issue of diversifying the faculty than to *be a member of* any protected class or minority group. This diversity advocate provides regular reminders of the importance of diversity at the institution, the availability of highly qualified minority candidates, and the need for the committee to avoid becoming so focused on academic credentials that it fails to see the full range of contributions that each applicant could bring to the position.

## ○ phrasing of the advertisement

The way in which notices about jobs are phrased can also affect the diversity of the applicant pool. As we saw previously, it's not uncommon to encounter advertisements stating "Women and minorities are welcome to apply." or even "An affirmative action/equal employment opportunity employer." But phrases like these have very little value (see Buller, 2015, p. 94). They may, in fact, be counterproductive by conveying the impression that the institution is doing the bare minimum to meet legal requirements about diversity. To potential applicants, stock formulae don't feel particularly inviting. To the contrary, they come across as cold and legalistic. Far more useful would be a statement that explains *why* the institution is committed to diversity or that *invites* the applicant to discuss a commitment to diversity in his or her application.

The Office for Faculty Equity & Welfare at the University of California, Berkeley outlines a number of ways in which advertisements for faculty positions can better address the institution's interest in diversifying its faculty. Among the statements it recommends are the following:

- The school/department seeks candidates whose research, teaching, or service has prepared them to contribute to our commitment to diversity and inclusion in higher education.
- The school/department is interested in candidates who have engaged in service towards increasing the participation of individuals from groups historically under-represented in higher education.
- The school/department is interested in candidates who have an understanding of the barriers facing women and people of color in higher education.
- The school/department is interested in candidates who will bring to their research the perspective that comes from a non-traditional educational background or understanding of the experiences of those under-represented in higher education. (Adapted from Office for Faculty Equity & Welfare, n.d.)

The *Guide to Best Practices in Faculty Search and Hiring* developed by the provost's office at Columbia University also provides excellent models for how diversity statements in advertisements can be written so as to be more effective than the formulas commonly used by other schools.

- Columbia University is an affirmative action, equal opportunity employer. The University is dedicated to the goal of building a culturally diverse and pluralistic faculty and staff committed to teaching and working in a diverse environment, and strongly encourages applications from women, minorities, individuals with disabilities and veterans.
- Columbia University is an equal opportunity institution. Because the University is committed to building a broadly diverse educational environment, applicants may include in their cover letter information about how they will further this objective.
- Applicants are encouraged to describe in their letter of intent how their scholarship contributes to building and supporting diverse communities. (Columbia University Office of the Provost, n.d., p. 16)

Moreover, Columbia recommends combining these statements about diversity with others that provide candidates with a better understanding of the institution's culture and commitment to work-life balance.

- The department welcomes applications from individuals who may have had nontraditional career paths, or who may have taken time off for family reasons (e.g., children, caring for disabled or elderly family), or who have achieved excellence in careers outside of academia (e.g., in professional or industry service).
- Columbia is responsive to the needs of dual career couples. (Columbia University Office of the Provost, n.d., p. 14)

> Job announcements often provide the first impression that a candidate has of an institution, so it's important when setting ambitious goals for diversity to phrase advertisements in a way that advances, not hinders, progress toward that goal.

## ○ targeted efforts

As important as are all the efforts we've discussed so far, most of them remain passive in nature. They are based on the assumption that, if you take certain steps, the right candidates will find you. But achieving an institution's diversity goals also often requires active interventions, steps that can help put you in contact with highly qualified candidates from protected classes. Among the most effective practices in targeting a diverse pool of applicants are the following:

- *Historically Black colleges and universities (HBCUs).* Even though the origins of Black colleges and universities are often associated with systematic discrimination at US institutions of higher education, many minority students still find these schools to be welcoming and highly supportive learning environments. As a result, universities such as Howard, Hampton, Florida A&M, and others graduate a significant number of minority students each year from their PhD programs. By building a constructive relationship with one or more of these institutions, you'll learn about students who will soon receive their terminal degrees, and you may thus have an opportunity to let them know about current employment possibilities. You can follow a similar strategy with respect to women's colleges for fields that have been traditionally dominated by men. Most women's colleges do not, however, grant terminal degrees (except, at times, the MFA), although a number of them do offer master's programs and, depending on the position you have available, could still be a good source of potential applicants.
- *Other institutions with highly diverse student populations.* Because of the importance of diversity in higher education, many colleges and universities have made efforts to attract a highly diverse student body. As a result, graduates of those institutions are familiar with working in a multicultural educational environment and more likely than graduates at many other schools to come from under-represented groups themselves. *U.S. News & World Report* maintains

annual lists of highly diverse colleges and universities—broken down by the schools' focus as a national university, regional university, liberal arts college, or regional college—that are producing the sort of potential faculty members you may want to interview for available positions (see *U.S. News & World Report*, 2016). Similar to HBCUs, these highly diverse institutions could become valuable partners with colleges and universities that are trying to diversify their faculties by providing advance notice of available jobs to current graduate students.

- *Minority caucuses in professional organizations.* Certain professional organizations either exist primarily for members of minority groups or have committees or caucuses within them that address issues of concern to women and minorities. The Office of Human Resources at the University of Chicago has developed a comprehensive website of these groups (see University of Chicago Human Resources, n.d.). The organizations and caucuses included on the list are eager to provide information about employment opportunities to their members, and so including them when distributing notices of faculty vacancies can help you reach new and experienced academic professionals.

- *Conferences designed for protected classes.* There are also annual institutes, conferences, and workshops for minority students and faculty members that can help provide the search committee with useful contacts. These events include meetings of the American Association of Blacks in Higher Education (www.blacksinhighered.org), the American Association of Hispanics in Higher Education (www.aahhe.org), the Annual Biomedical Research Conference for Minority Students (www.abrcms.org), and similar meetings. These conferences put search committees into contact with a broad network of qualified faculty members, and some of them even offer job-posting boards and opportunities to interview or prescreen potential candidates.

- *Targeted publications and websites.* Certain sources of information about faculty vacancies are designed for use by minorities and women.

Search committees need to exert a certain degree of caution because unscrupulous publishers have been known to develop journals and newsletters that claim to be intended primarily for women and minorities in higher education, charge high prices for advertisements, and have a very low circulation rate. In general, it's best to rely on publications and websites that have a well-established track record, such as *Diverse Issues in Higher Education* (diverseeducation.com), *The Journal of Blacks in Higher Education* (www.jbhe.com), *Latinos in Higher Education* (www.latinosinhighered.com), and *Women in Higher Education* (wihe.com).

- *Programs at other institutions.* It's generally considered to be poor practice to raid other departments of their minority or female faculty members. Nevertheless, there are occasions when you might learn of a faculty member at another institution who is being underused or placed in a position that doesn't take full advantage of his or her capabilities. In these cases, it's not inappropriate to make sure that that person at least knows about any positions you have available. Whether or not he or she applies, of course, is entirely that person's choice.

- *Your own undergraduate students.* Finally, even though it's a long-term strategy, institutions might think about encouraging their own female and minority graduate students to pursue a career in higher education. By providing fellowships to qualified candidates—perhaps with the expectation that the recipient would then serve on the faculty for a certain period of time—colleges and universities can help diversify their own faculty by transforming the talented undergraduates of today into the professors of tomorrow.

## ○ the positive and negative aspects of fit

At several points throughout this book, I address the importance of identifying a candidate who has the right fit for your program and institution. But when it comes to faculty searches, people sometimes use the word *fit* in two very different ways. The first way, which is how I'll be using this word whenever it appears, has to do with finding someone who matches what a program *needs*. That need could be a matter of the person's academic discipline, but it could also relate to other highly desirable qualities, areas of experience, and points of view that the candidate can contribute so as to make the program and institution better. The second way of using the word *fit*, which often proves to make it just a euphemism for discrimination, is to regard *fit* as implying "people like us." That's not the kind of fit I ever mean in this book. In fact, candidates who have the right fit in the first sense of the word—bringing to the program a number of important contributions that it needs— often run counter to the second sense of the word. Many times, what our programs and institutions need are people who are decidedly *not* like us, because we can benefit from introducing faculty members whose background, experiences, and pedagogical approach can better address the requirements of an ever-evolving body of students.

It's useful, therefore, for members of a search committee to have a serious conversation about what they as a group mean by the word *fit* at the very beginning of the process. This practice helps prevent institutions from eliminating candidates for reasons such as "she or he just won't fit in here" or "I just don't see him or her as a good fit with the close-knit group we've developed in our department." When people make these remarks, they almost always do so with the best intentions. But, if the assumptions behind them go unchallenged, the pursuit of the wrong kind of fit can undo all your other efforts to achieve diversity for your program.

## ○ putting it all together

As one way of seeing where you stand with regard to faculty diversity, we're going to end this chapter with an exercise that involves the following groups:

- The faculty in each major specialty area within your department or program (such as Spanish, Japanese, and Arabic within a department of foreign languages or North American, South American, European, African, and Asian history within a department of history)
- The faculty of the department or program as a whole

- The faculty of the college or division
- The students at the institution
- The faculty, staff, and administration of the institution
- The general population of the city or region in which the institution is located

Once you've identified these groups, take an inventory of each of them, to the best of your ability, in terms of their breakdown in terms of which are defined as protected classes according to your institution's nondiscrimination statement, your state laws, and federal laws. As you examine this distribution, where are the outliers, the groups in which the distribution of protected classes is noticeably different from the others? For example, you may find that the gender balance of the student body is significantly different from that of the faculty in the department, or that the general population of the city is far more racially diverse than the faculty in one of your department's academic specialties. Having this information can serve as an important first step in guiding you toward where you may need to focus your efforts at diversifying the faculty when you define positions and conduct searches.

# 2

# advertising the position

The Internet has changed how institutions recruit and how potential faculty members find available positions. In the 1980s and 1990s when we were searching for new colleagues, we'd advertise the position by placing a notice in *The Chronicle of Higher Education,* one or two professional journals, and perhaps a publication that was designed primarily for minority candidates. Now we may well take those same steps but also realize that we'll have to be much more proactive if we want to attract the best pool of applicants to fit our needs. As we saw in the last chapter, diversifying a candidate pool usually requires long-term recruitment tools such as building relationships with organizations and institutions that are likely to have a sizable number of qualified minority candidates and conducting prescreening sessions at conferences that tend to attract a diverse group of participants. In addition, many people don't even consult print journals about possible openings anymore, so search committees have to adopt the mind-set of candidates in order to know where to post their advertisements. Finally, taking all of these steps can be time-consuming and expensive, so cost-benefit analysis has to come into play to make sure that the institution's advertising efforts bring it the best results for the resources it has available.

Best practices in recruiting faculty members suggest that effective advertisement of positions usually involves a five-step process:

1. Decide what information the most desirable and qualified candidates need to know in order to be encouraged to apply for the position.
2. Decide on the most appropriate venues for disseminating that information.
3. Tailor the information to the specific venue.
4. Track success rates of each venue and advertisement format to improve future searches.
5. Adjust the strategy as needed if the desired results aren't being obtained.

Because each of these steps involves making a number of decisions that may be different in any individual search, let's explore each of them in a bit more detail.

○ step one: decide what information the most desirable and qualified candidates need to know in order to be encouraged to apply for the position

In order to determine what information you need to provide in an advertisement to increase the likelihood of finding the best possible person for the job, you have to begin by asking the same questions you were probably taught in Rhetoric 101:

• Who is my audience?
• What is the outcome I'd most like to receive from my audience?
• What type of message is most likely to result in that sort of outcome from that sort of audience?

If most search committees consider these questions at all, they probably do so only superficially. For instance, some people may not give these issues any more consideration than as shown in the following examples:

- Who is my audience? *People with advanced degrees who are looking for a job*
- What is the outcome I'd most like to receive from my audience? *That these people apply for this job*
- What type of message is most likely to induce that sort of outcome from that sort of audience? *Information about the job and how to apply for it*

That limited type of analysis is unlikely to result in advertising that has any significant impact. There's no consideration given to the level of experience a candidate is expected to have. Is this an entry-level position for someone just completing graduate school, an eminent scholar position for a distinguished senior member of the faculty, or a position that falls somewhere in between? You need to know the level of the position because different types of candidates will expect different sorts of information, in different venues, and possibly at different times during the academic year. If you don't probe a little further into what the expectations are, you could end up with a pool of vastly overqualified applicants that your school couldn't possibly afford or a pool of highly inexperienced candidates who really aren't up to the requirements of the job. It's more efficient to ask the right questions at the beginning than to waste time sifting through dozens of irrelevant applications and then possibly be compelled to extend or cancel the search because the original advertisement wasn't properly crafted. So, let's look into these questions a bit more deeply.

## Who Is My Audience?

What this question is really asking can be paraphrased as follows:

- What are the best-qualified applicants for this position likely to already know or assume about the job itself, my institution, or the area in which this institution is located?
- How much experience do we expect our leading candidates to have?
- Are there likely to be other factors that our most desirable candidates might share?

- By shifting our focus in some way, might we have success in reaching a broader audience of competitive candidates who otherwise might not know or care about this position?

It's important to consider these issues because they lie at the very heart of a successful advertising strategy. Distinguished senior professors in your discipline sometimes don't read the same publications or visit the same websites as do graduate students. Your institution could be one with a name that's instantly recognizable (Harvard, Princeton, Yale); geographically confusing to people who aren't familiar with it (Miami University of Ohio, Indiana University of Pennsylvania, California University of Pennsylvania); or largely unknown to all but local candidates. Your position may have little to do with approaches such as game theory or big data analytics, but those approaches could be so central to what everyone else in the department does that a successful candidate would need at least some basic familiarity with them. In general, you want to try to picture the type of people your best applicant pool will contain, what they will know, what they might assume, and what they will need to learn and do in order to succeed in the position.

## What Is the Outcome I'd Most Like to Receive From My Audience?

Naturally you'd like a highly qualified candidate to apply for your position, but are there other steps that he or she may need or want to take before getting to that point? The questions you need to ask yourself about what you'd like your audience to do can best be summarized as follows:

- Is there a website with more information you'd like the reader of the ad to examine?
- Are there printed materials you'd like to send potential applicants in order to provide more information about the position, school, or region?
- Is the position so specialized that it's better for a potential candidate to speak with a representative of the program to determine whether it's even worthwhile to apply for the job?

If the position or your institution is so attractive that you'll probably receive several hundred applications, you don't want that number to increase with inquiries from people who aren't serious or even remotely qualified for the job. For this reason, it may be desirable to set up some hurdles for candidates to clear to ensure that those screened by the committee deserve the time this process might require. The hurdles you create should be in line with the nature of the position itself. For example, if the position is heavily teaching oriented, require the candidate to submit a 1,000-word philosophy-of-teaching statement that addresses issues such as specific strategies for promoting active learning, increasing student engagement in large classes, and the most effective design for a hybrid (combined in-person and online) course. By making the prompt as specific as possible, you reduce the likelihood that applicants simply will recycle the same philosophy of teaching statement they include with every application. If the position is heavily research-oriented and designed for a senior scholar, ask applicants to submit a copy of their most recent book or a list of externally funded grants worth more than a million dollars.

However, your position may be one that's likely to attract a relatively small pool of applicants. In that case, you want to make it very easy to apply for the position. You may also wish to provide information that can help turn potential applicants into actual applicants. For example, it may be the case that your institution isn't particularly well known or located in a very remote area. Inducements for people to apply might include an address (short and easy to remember) for a website that includes more information about the department and position as well as appealing videos of nearby beaches, ski resorts, or national parks, all conveniently located near the campus. If you're uncertain what strategies might be effective, take a look at what your school's office of admissions uses to attract prospective students. Often you'll find that that some of their approaches (and possibly even some of their electronic or printed materials) are equally well suited to encourage prospective job applicants to apply.

## What Type of Message Is Most Likely to Induce That Sort of Outcome From That Sort of Audience?

If your target pool of applicants is unlikely to know much about your institution, you'll need to introduce them to the school before you can even begin to introduce them to the position. If your desired pool of applicants is likely to have negative preconceived notions of the region where you're located, you'll need to point out its positive attributes before they'll consider investigating further. If your position is different from others commonly found in your field—perhaps because it combines two disciplines that are usually distinct but that are both required for the duties of this job—you'll need to explain what the position entails before potential applicants can see themselves succeeding at the task. Make no mistake about it: Even if you don't take any of these steps, you'll probably still have applicants for the position. But they may not be the *best* applicants you could possibly attract. So, before drafting a position announcement or job advertisement, put yourself in the place of the most competitive applicants you can imagine for the position: What will they need to know about the area, institution, program, and position in order to think, "I'd like to have this job"? Let your answer to that question guide you in framing the content for your advertisement.

Finally, remember what we've already said several times about diversifying the candidate pool. Simply ending an announcement with phrases such as "Women and minorities encouraged to apply" or "An affirmative action/equal employment opportunity institution" isn't likely to bring you that rich pool of candidates from many different backgrounds that you'd like. In fact, these phrases may even be somewhat counterproductive. They give the appearance that the institution is merely going through the motions of claiming that diversity is important in faculty searches. After all, in the current social climate, if you have to say that you think diversity among the faculty is significant, maybe your school doesn't value it as much as you think.

It's always far better to include a statement about *why* faculty diversity is important at your school than one that simply claims it's important.

○   step two: decide on the most appropriate venues
    for disseminating that information

As we've seen, different audiences respond to different media. Distinguished senior professors, who may not be looking for a new job actively but could be attracted to the right opportunity if it came along, may read print journals and be on e-mail lists from professional organizations. They're probably not receiving links to (or at least not regularly looking at) websites that specialize in posting academic jobs. Graduate students who are about to enter the field are, however, probably scrutinizing these sites with great frequency, but they may be so busy completing their own research projects that they don't have enough time to peruse every article and advertisement that appears in professional journals. In some disciplines, print resources still dominate, whereas others have shifted almost entirely to electronic media. Some disciplines have a major conference where positions are posted and candidates are interviewed, and others prefer to keep the hiring process separate from the process of sharing scholarly developments. It's important to investigate how the sort of candidates you want to attract are most likely to learn about available jobs, particularly if the position is one that extends beyond the typical disciplinary borders of your field.

For this reason, the key questions a search committee needs to ask at this point in the process are the following:

- Which sources of information is my target audience likely to use the most?
- In what format is my target audience likely to use them?
- What are the most expeditious ways of getting that information to my target audience in that format?

In other words, even if you decide that the vast majority of your most desirable candidates are likely to look for new positions in *The Chronicle of Higher Education* and two or three professional journals in your field, your task still isn't done. *The Chronicle* offers print and electronic ads. So do most professional journals. Is your position one in which a person who's not really looking for a job might become interested in it if he or she just happened to find it? In that case, you may be better off focusing on print ads in publications that people tend to read regularly. In fact, if the position is important enough to your institution, you may want to invest in a print ad that appears among the articles at the front of the publication rather than among the other job notices at the end where your best candidates may not even consider looking.

Your decision might be very different if your position is for an instructor or entry-level assistant professor. Most of the candidates for those jobs are already actively involved in looking for work. They explore the online job sites regularly and probably receive e-mail alerts whenever a new position comes online. In this case, you may decide to save money by forgoing a print advertisement entirely and placing your efforts solely in the area of electronic communications. The yield isn't likely to be very different than if you had purchased print ads, and those resources could be better channeled to other ways of getting the word out, such as writing letters to directors of graduate programs in your field or attending a conference in your discipline and posting flyers on the notice board. In fact, many search committees find that their most productive source of highly qualified applicants comes from their relationships with directors of graduate programs that produce large numbers of qualified candidates in that field. Although these relationships can take time to develop, they're worth the investment because the applicants they produce will come from programs that you know well and that have taken the time to understand your department's focus and needs.

One mistake search committees sometimes make is directing their advertising efforts solely toward disciplinary organizations with a fairly narrow focus. It's important to remember that there are many different kinds of professional organizations that can help you get your message to the right pool of candidates. For example, does the position involve promoting or mentoring undergraduate research? If so, then the Council on Undergraduate Research (www.cur.org) might also be an appropriate venue for your search announcements. Will the faculty member be involved in honors education? If so, then it may be wise to send a listing to the National Collegiate Honors Council (www.nchchonors.org). Will the position involve graduate education? Consider working with the Council of Graduate Schools (www.cgsnet.org).

When creating advertisements for academic positions, think about the position holistically. Ask what else the faculty member will be doing *in addition to* teaching and conducting research within your field's disciplinary boundaries. Those additional duties may provide keys to where you should place your advertisements and what should be included in them.

## ○ step three: tailor the information to the specific venue

Professional journals sometimes have requirements (or at least guidelines or traditions) about how position announcements should be structured and phrased. Online sites may have specific data fields in which information must be entered and which then structure the announcement in a particular way. These requirements mean that search announcements at times must be adapted to meet the rules of a publisher. But there are also other concerns search committees will want to keep in mind when planning their advertisements for individual sites and publications. We've already seen, for example, that senior scholars may be gathering information from different sources than people who are seeking their first or second academic appointment. In a similar way, different applicants may also care about different things. A graduate student who will just be starting out as a faculty member will probably care most about long-term security and the possibility for advancement, so the questions to consider include the following:

- Is this a permanent position?
- Does it offer the possibility of tenure or a multiyear contract?
- Will my research be supported in such a way that receiving tenure or a multiyear contract becomes more likely?
- Is promotion possible and, if so, after how many years?
- Is the institution family friendly?

Although it's possible that eminent scholars may also be interested in family-friendly environments and the security of the position, other issues may loom even larger for them:

- If I have an existing research team, can I bring them with me for this position?
- Will existing facilities be renovated if that's necessary for my research?
- Are bridge grants from the institution possible if I find myself between grants in a few years?
- What portion of indirect cost recovery on grants does the institution return to principal investigators?
- What are the special benefits and privileges that the institution provides its distinguished research professors?

An easy mistake to make in searches is, therefore, to develop a single generic advertisement or position announcement and then use it for every publication, website, and mailing connected with the search. You should always consider who will be seeing the announcement in any particular venue, what he or she will need to know in order to become interested in the position, and how the text can be focused on those priorities in order to be most effective.

> An old journalistic principle is "Don't bury the lede," meaning that it's a poor practice to make the reader go through multiple sentences or paragraphs to reach the most important information. The most significant details should come first, in job announcements just as in news stories.

If your position will allow the successful candidate to hire additional faculty members as part of a research team, is accompanied by a significant amount of travel funding, represents a major new initiative of the school's strategic plan, or allows the successful candidate to plan the program's curriculum, then it's a good idea to place that information at the very beginning of the advertisement. It may induce the perfect pool of applicants to read an ad that they may have ignored if it simply began "Tenure-track assistant professor in [discipline]" or in some other formulaic manner.

◦ step four: track success rates of each venue and advertisement format to improve future searches

In fact, if you wanted to conduct an experiment to determine the effectiveness of creating announcements with the most important information first, you might consider running your advertisement in two different formats. For two weeks, have the position announced on a job website with fairly standard phrasing: tenure status, rank, and discipline first, then starting date, then additional details about the position. The following two weeks include the same information but structure it differently so that the most distinctive aspect of the position is listed first. For example, an ad might begin "Opportunity to be in on the ground floor of a new program in complex systems" or "Teach and conduct research at a university *The Chronicle* has profiled in its 'Best Colleges to Work For' issue for 8 consecutive years." Then see which version of the ad brings you more results in general, more results from qualified candidates, or more results from the most competitive candidates. In most cases you'll find that the second format is far more effective.

This type of experiment, known as *A/B testing*, is done in commercial advertising all the time. In fact, your school's office of admissions may do its own A/B testing when it tries out new recruitment materials, varies the colors used in its e-mail marketing, alters the order of the information a message contains, experiments with different subject lines in e-mails, and so on. Colleges and universities are usually behind the curve when it comes to adopting this practice for faculty searches, however, even though most people would argue that an institution is judged at least as much by the quality of its faculty as the quality of its students (probably more). By learning which venues and advertisement formats are most effective in bringing you the type of applicant pool you want, you'll not only have valuable information for adjusting your advertising strategies in mid-search (the next topic that we'll consider) but also be better prepared for future searches. You'll know which journals tend to net the largest number of applicants in various categories (total, qualified, and highly competitive); which are most useful in diversifying the pool; which bring you the candidates that you're most likely to interview and eventually hire; and how much each advertising effort cost you per applicant. Armed with that information, you'll thus be in a far better position to devote your time and budget to their most effective uses in the future.

You can track the impact of your advertising efforts in various ways. The most common device used by institutions is to include a reply survey card to each applicant in the letter that states that his or her application has been received. These survey cards typically have the applicant check a few boxes indicating how he or she learned of the position and then mail back the card postage paid. The problem is that reply survey cards often have a very low response rate, so other approaches may be more useful. With online job listings, the link that takes a potential candidate to the job application will probably provide the school with an indication of where the applicant found the electronic listing. For print publications, you may need to be a bit creative. For instance, you could include a different code in the address to which the applicant mails his or her materials for each venue in which the advertisement appears. If the candidate mails an application to an address containing the code "ATTN: Office CHE," you'd know he or she was responding to an ad in *The Chronicle of Higher Education*. If, however, the address was written in a way that included the code "ATTN: Office JPS," you'd know he or she was responding to an ad in the *Journal of Pedestrian Studies*, and so on. You can achieve this goal even more subtly simply by modifying the middle initial of the search chair. Those sending their applications to "Magnanimous C. Search-chair" must have seen the ad in *The Chronicle*, those who address their applications to "Magnanimous W. Searchchair" must be looking at the department's website, and so on.

For electronic communications, a number of online tools also help you track this information. With Google Analytics, you can perform A/B testing of different ads or e-mails very easily, determine where your applicants tend to be located (as well as people who may read the advertisement but fail to complete the application), what times of day and days of the week bring you the best responses, what other pages on your school's website potential applicants tend to visit, how long people remain on your website, and who revisits the site frequently. Although setting up these features requires a bit of technical expertise, it isn't particularly difficult and can provide you with hard data by which you can refine your advertisement strategies.

o    ## step five: adjust the strategy as needed if the desired results aren't being obtained

Unless you're conducting a search with a very short deadline, your system for tracking the effectiveness of various forms of your search announcement can help you improve the process even while applications are still coming in. For example, if you learn that the form of your ad that starts by mentioning the amount of research funding available at the institution is yielding three times the number of applications as the form of your ad that begins by mentioning the rank and discipline of the position, you'll know how you should structure any subsequent ads so as to have the greatest impact. If you learn that websites are yielding 90% of your applications, and letters and print ads are bringing you only 10%, you can adapt your recruitment strategy midcourse in order to maximize your effectiveness. Of course, numbers of applications alone aren't the only factors to consider. It could well be that most of the applicants who responded to your letters and print ads are highly competitive whereas only a handful of those responding to websites meet your minimum qualifications. Nevertheless, faculty recruitment and hiring always take place in an environment of limited resources. There's never enough time to interview all the candidates you'd like to meet and never enough money to advertise everywhere you desire your notices to be seen. Tracking your results as the search unfolds rather than looking at the pool only after the deadline has passed thus helps the search committee make the best use of its efforts. It also reduces the likelihood that the search will need to be extended or aborted because it resulted in an insufficient pool of applicants.

Although tracking these results on an ongoing basis is a good practice, it's sometimes beneficial not to screen the applications too closely as they arrive. It can be tempting to become preoccupied with an early application that strikes you as exceptional and then to use that application as a touchstone for all others, thus disadvantaging a number of highly qualified candidates who happened to apply a little later. For example, in a search for an organic chemist, you might notice that an early applicant is fluent in Russian and see the advantage this skill would have in assisting your program with its ongoing collaboration with Lomonosov Moscow State University. Then, even though fluency in Russian was never stated as a requirement or even a preferred qualification for your position, you might start disregarding other highly competitive candidates just because they don't have an attribute you hadn't even thought of before reading that one impressive application. For this reason, it's a good idea to track applications as they come in only in the following terms:

- Is the application complete? In other words, did the candidate submit all the materials that you requested?
- Is the candidate qualified? In other words, does the candidate meet every criterion you publicly described as a requirement?
- Is the candidate highly competitive? In other words, does the candidate meet one or more criterion that you publicly described as a preference?

## o  Frequently Asked Questions About Search Advertisements

Because position announcements and search advertisements often have to be condensed because of their cost, search committees sometimes wonder about the importance of including specific types of information in the ad. They may also wonder about the best way of phrasing certain requirements, preferences, or aspects of the position. The following are a few best practices related to these frequently asked questions.

## How Should the Issue of Rank Be Handled?

It may not seem as though an issue as clear-cut as the successful candidate's academic rank could be very problematic, but search committees often struggle over how to discuss rank in an ad. For example, if an advertisement states that a program is searching for an assistant professor, would it be possible later to hire someone as an associate or full professor if he or she met the qualifications for this rank? (Answer: It depends on your institution. Some schools are quite flexible in deviating from the text of the ad, and others insist that, if the advertisement was seeking an assistant professor, the successful candidate can *only* be given the rank of assistant professor. It may also be the case that there simply isn't sufficient funding to support the salary of someone at a higher rank.) Would highly desirable associate or full professors be dissuaded from applying for a position if the rank is listed as assistant professor? (Answer: Probably. They're likely to assume that the institution is not seeking or could not afford someone of higher rank.) So, best practices suggest the following.

> If rank is going to be mentioned in an ad, the text should reflect the exact degree of flexibility the school has.

If the matter is truly open, then saying something such as "rank dependent on qualifications" is your best option; otherwise, describe the situation precisely, using such phrases as "tenure-eligible assistant professor," "assistant or associate professor," "distinguished professor," and the like.

## How Should the Issue of Contract Status Be Handled?

Most potential applicants regard contract status as second in importance only to salary in determining whether to apply for a job. Someone who's desperate for employment, someone who recently received a doctorate and wants a year or two of experience in order to gain a competitive edge, or someone who is place-bound in your area may not care that a position is a 1-year sabbatical replacement or of otherwise short duration. But most other highly qualified candidates are unlikely to be interested in relocating for a position that has no chance of becoming long term. Certainly, if your position is tenure-track, eligible for a multiyear contract, or holds the possibility of tenure being granted (usually to distinguished or eminent scholars) on hiring, it's a good idea to feature that fact prominently in your announcement. That level of security is a powerful incentive for highly qualified applicants to apply. But if your position is temporary, it's only fair to mention that fact as well (although perhaps not as prominently). It would be a waste of time for the candidate and your committee to go through the search process with someone who almost certainly wouldn't accept the position if it were offered.

> A general rule of thumb for contract status is always to include a reference to tenure eligibility (or your institution's equivalent) in the advertisement but draw attention to it only if it is likely to be an incentive for candidates to apply.

### Should the Salary Range Be Mentioned in the Advertisement?

There are two schools of thought about this issue. One school says that you should never mention salary in an advertisement because, if you do, you then become locked into that range and may end up discouraging some candidates to whom that salary may seem low (perhaps because they don't understand that the cost of living in your area is also lower than in many metropolitan areas). The other school says that, if you have a set range, it's better to make that clear up front. Just as the search committee shouldn't have to waste time reviewing a candidate who wouldn't seriously consider taking a temporary position, so should it not have to devote time to reviewing a candidate who wouldn't accept a position at that salary. Besides, the second group might argue, a high-enough salary could well be an inducement for certain candidates to apply. The middle ground that many institutions end up occupying is to say "salary dependent on qualifications," a relatively meaningless phrase that tells potential applicants next to nothing and simply takes up space in the ad.

> Mentioning salary in a search advertisement is likely to cause more problems later than simply ignoring the issue of compensation completely.

In the United States specifying a salary in an advertisement is particularly unwise if the institution ends up hiring a foreign national on an H visa. When the faculty member later applies for permanent residency, an advertised salary that is lower than the government's prevailing wage determination for that type of position could require the institution to readvertise the position; if that happens and a citizen with credentials comparable to those of the foreign national applies when the position is readvertised, the institution may not be allowed to retain the foreign national. (For more on this issue, see also, Buller, 2015, pp. 402–403.) As a result, best practices indicate that you should not discuss salary in a search advertisement; discuss that issue during interviews with semifinalists or finalists, but don't include it in the ad.

### Should the Degree Required for the Position Be Mentioned in the Advertisement?

Before attempting to answer this question, search committees need to ask about this issue in a different way: What are the minimum acceptable credentials that are necessary for someone to be qualified to hold this position? Accrediting agencies regularly expect institutions to develop clear standards for faculty qualifications. Often those requirements will be a minimum of 18 graduate credit hours in courses closely related to the discipline the faculty member is teaching, a significant record of peer-reviewed research in that discipline, or an equivalent level of professional experience other than teaching. (That last stipulation is important because many accrediting agencies will not conclude that a faculty member is qualified to teach a course merely because he or she has already taught it for many years.) Admittedly it's rare to see an advertisement that includes a phrase such as "requirements include a minimum of 18 graduate credit hours of course work in the discipline(s) closely associated with this position," but it might be better if the practice were more widespread. Other types of statements tend to cause problems. As we've already seen, if you say "PhD required," your institution may or may not allow you to hire someone with a EdD, PsyD, DA, or any other type of doctorate; similar to salary, that level of specificity in the ad may also cause you problems if a foreign national hired on a H visa later applies for permanent residency in the United States. If you say "doctorate required," you may not be able to hire someone who hasn't yet defended his or dissertation or who has a master's degree but 12 highly acclaimed books on the topic. Moreover, these phrases are ambiguous: *When* is the degree required? At the time of application? At the time of hiring? Before the first year of the contract is complete? It may not seem like very eloquent phrasing, but the best practice to follow is to include a statement such as "prior to being issued a contract, the successful candidate must demonstrate that he or she fully meets the [relevant accrediting body's] credentialing requirements for faculty." Such a statement gives the committee the greatest amount of flexibility in choosing a qualified candidate but also establishes a relevant set of credentialing requirements and a deadline by which those requirements must be met. If candidates are unsure as to whether they meet those requirements, they can contact the search chair. That type of contact gives the chair an additional opportunity to persuade a highly competitive candidate to apply and to dissuade an unqualified candidate from wasting his or her time (as well as the time that would be spent by the committee).

## Should the Starting Date of the Position Be Indicated?

If there is a firm date by which the successful applicant's presence on campus will be required, then the starting date of the contract should be indicated. Doing so prevents the search process from getting all the way to the hiring stage before finding out that its preferred candidate has other obligations that prevent him or her from starting the position when needed. If the starting date is flexible, including that information in the ad might be an inducement for certain candidates to apply, but otherwise there is little reason to include it.

## Should a Required or Preferred Level of Experience Be Indicated?

Although it's common to see phrases such as "3 years of experience required" in search advertisements, these statements frequently cause more problems than they solve. After all, what kind of experience are you looking for? Teaching experience? If so, does it have to be at the college level or would a person with 3 years of teaching at a highly selective private high school qualify? Or do you mean research experience? If so, does that research experience have to be at a university or major research lab, or does the applicant's 3 years of undergraduate research count? If you mean any kind of experience, then who doesn't have at least 3 years of experience in *something* (life? employment of any kind? study within the discipline?)? And would you really not want to hire that otherwise highly qualified and competitive candidate who only has 2 years and 9 months of whatever kind of experience you specify? It doesn't make the matter any better to say something similar to "3 years of university-level teaching experience preferred" because the word *preferred* is open to so many interpretations. One member of the search committee might argue that any candidate who meets that specification must automatically be given preference over any candidate who doesn't. Another member of the search committee will argue that preferences only come into play when trying to decide between two candidates who are otherwise equally qualified. And yet another member of the search committee will argue that the phrase was intended only to provide guidance to possible applicants, not to serve as any sort of litmus test. Because ad space is always at a premium, best practices suggest that leaving out all references to a desired level of experience, regardless of whether it is called a requirement or a preference, is highly desirable.

## Should Information About the Institution Be Included in the Ad?

As we saw previously, answering this question requires you to know who your audience is likely to be. If your school is so little known that a candidate may not even investigate the position further unless he or she knows something more about it, then a brief statement about the institution may well be worth including. What you say need not be long. For example, a name such as Smallville State College may make the school seem remote to someone unfamiliar with the area. In that case, you might want to include a line such as "located within a short driving distance of the thriving cultural capital of Metropolis, Smallville State College offers the personal touch of a friendly community plus the lifestyle amenities of a major city." More detail can be provided on the school's website for faculty positions, so you only need a brief phrase that counteracts any misconception a potential applicant may have. If your institution is one that has instant (and positive) name recognition, then including this type of information merely wastes space.

## What Requirements Apply to an Ad That Is to Be Used for Permanent Residency ("Green Card") Purposes?

If you hire a foreign national who does not have permanent residency status, the labor certification process of the US federal government requires that the advertisement for the position meet certain requirements. If those requirements aren't met by the original version of the ad, you may be required to repost the position. Because reposting requires that you conduct a bona fide search and not merely go through the motions of doing so, there is always a possibility that the foreign national will not be hired as a result of the later process. For this reason, it's better to follow the federal requirements for ads that meet the labor certification guidelines even when you don't anticipate hiring a foreign national. Your best candidate may well turn out to be a noncitizen without permanent residency status, and you'll save yourself problems down the line if you meet the requirements from the beginning.

In order for a job advertisement to meet the US federal requirements for use in a labor certification process, the ad must follow these stipulations:

- Be publicly posted for at least 30 calendar days with the start and end dates of the posting clearly documented

> • Be placed in a national professional journal (in print or online) targeted at an appropriate audience for higher education positions as opposed to a general purpose national website

Posting an advertisement in *The Chronicle of Higher Education's* print version and making the online ad available on *The Chronicle's* website meets these requirements; posting the position in your break room or on Monster.com for 10 days does not.

## ○ putting it all together

If you include in the advertisement everything that you think an applicant could possibly want to know about the position, the resulting text will be too expensive to post and too dense for many applicants to read. That's why the five-step process outlined in this chapter is so useful. As you think about what possible applicants might need to know, you'll end up creating a raw source file that can be modified and tailored for different purposes. From that file, you can adapt the information to meet the style guidelines of specific publications or websites. You can select different sorts of information depending on what will matter the most to the audience of any given journal or electronic publication. The goal then is to draw from your source file the specific items that the people who consult each individual website or publication are likely to care about most and then order them in a manner that captures the attention of the reader and directs that reader to a source of additional information. The candidates who want your advertised position will be giving a great deal of attention to how they might make you interested in them. Your goal in developing your search advertisements should be to devote at least as much attention to how you might make them interested in you.

# 3

# reviewing the applications

Once the application deadline has passed, it's time for the search committee to begin reviewing the applications in order to select a short list of semifinalists who will receive further examination. But before proceeding to this stage, it's important to recognize that the term *deadline* is used in several different ways in academic searches. First, it might be used in the strict sense: In order to be eligible for consideration, a candidate's application must be submitted (or in some cases *received*) by the deadline date. Once the deadline is reached, no new applications will be considered. Usually, the strict sense of the word *deadline* is interpreted as requiring that at least part of the application, such as a letter of interest or a nomination by a third party, must have a postmark on or before the deadline date or be time-stamped as an electronic submission on or before the deadline date. But sometimes institutions adopt an even stricter policy by requiring that a candidate's application be *complete* (i.e., that all necessary documents arrive for the search committee's consideration) by the deadline date.

The second sense of the term *deadline* is far more forgiving: It suggests that there is a *priority deadline*. Applications will begin to be reviewed soon after the date indicated, but additional applications will still be accepted until the position is filled. At some institutions, applications arriving before the priority deadline will be given preference over those that arrive later. At other institutions, all applications are treated equally regardless of when they were submitted. Because the way in which deadlines are treated is usually a matter of institutional policy, be sure you understand how your college or university uses this word before you begin to review the applications.

Even if your institution does not have a policy on how deadlines must be handled for all searches, the way in which your advertisements were written may have indicated how your search committee should approach the deadline date. For example, your advertisements may have included a phrase similar to one of the following:

- In order to be eligible for consideration, all materials required for the application must be postmarked (or *received* or *electronically submitted*) by [date].
- In order to be eligible for consideration, a letter of interest must be postmarked (or *received* or *electronically submitted*) by [date] with all remaining materials submitted to the search committee within 2 weeks of that date.
- Review of applications will begin on [date], but applications will continue to be received and reviewed until the position is filled.
- Priority will be given to applications postmarked (or *received* or *electronically submitted*) by [date], but applications will continue to be received and reviewed until the position is filled.

Including language of this kind when a job is advertised is a benefit to everyone. It provides guidance to the search committee and potential applicants about how the published deadline for the search will be enforced and how applications received after that deadline will be handled.

In their eagerness to begin reviewing applications, search committees sometimes neglect to notify qualified applicants about any materials that are missing from their applications. Although this oversight is often unintentional, there may also be search committee members who argue that it is the candidate's responsibility to make sure that his or her portfolio is complete, not the responsibility of the search committee to track down missing materials. Valid arguments can be made on both sides of this issue, but it's useful to remember that applicants aren't always aware of whether their references have submitted the letters of recommendation they agreed to write. Moreover, even if the incomplete application is the candidate's fault, ignoring an otherwise highly competitive candidate because he or she misread the list of required items in an advertisement is probably not in the institution's long-term best interests.

> Best practices in faculty recruitment and hiring suggest that giving applicants every opportunity to make their strongest possible case helps yield the most competitive and diverse pool of candidates.

## ○  best practices for chairs of search committees

As the search committee prepares to review the applications, it's helpful for the chair of the search committee to review with committee members some basic procedures so as to ensure fairness throughout the process and increase the likelihood of selecting the best applicant. Among some of the principles to consider when charging the committee are the following:

- The first test to use when evaluating candidates should be whether an applicant meets the basic requirements for the position. If someone is clearly not qualified—that is, he or she does not possess one or more of the qualifications designated as *required* in the search announcement—it would be a waste of the committee's time to consider that applicant further because it won't be possible to hire that person anyway. At this point in the discussion, you may want to review for the committee how your institution interprets various requirements in search advertisements. For example, Chapter 2 shares that some schools won't permit a program to hire an applicant with a PsyD or EdD if the advertisement reads "PhD required," and some won't permit a program to hire a candidate as an associate professor if the advertisement specifically states another rank. For this reason, clarifying for the committee the degree of flexibility allowed at your institution will make their task easier and help avoid disagreements later in the process.

- It's also useful to clarify how the committee should apply its professional judgment in cases when the evidence isn't clear. For example, if an advertisement reads "doctorate required by the starting date of the contract," and an applicant began his or her doctoral work only a month ago, members will need to decide whether they believe it's feasible for the candidate to complete the degree in the time available. In a similar way, if the person you hire must be able to teach a certain course, and an applicant has taught courses only in different areas of your discipline, the members of the committee will need to use their professional knowledge (as well as their understanding of their own school's procedures) to determine whether that person could be credentialed to teach the course in question.

- Chapter 2 also describes how listing preferences in a search advertisement can frequently complicate rather than clarify the search process. Search committees often get into disagreements over how to handle preferred qualifications: Should candidates with those qualifications receive guaranteed priority over those who lack them? Should preferences be considered only when deciding between two candidates who are otherwise very similar in background? Should they be ignored entirely during an initial screening? It's a good practice to come to a consensus about how your committee will treat preferred qualifications very early in the selection process so that everyone proceeds with the same understanding. If you wait until later to have this conversation, members of the search committee may already have formed opinions about the desirability of certain candidates and be unwilling to alter those opinions even if they run counter to your own view about how preferences should be handled.

That problem can be avoided if the discussion about preferred qualifications is held before anyone has even seen the applications, and the principles you are discussing are merely matters of general strategy rather than practical decisions that give advantage or disadvantage to specific applicants.

- This initial conversation with the search committee is also a good time to discuss how your group will rank the different priorities for the position. Searches often begin with a fairly long wish list of what the program hopes to find in the person it will hire, but not all the items on that list will be of equal importance. Naturally, different people on the committee will have different views about the relative priority of certain items—that's one of the major reasons for using a committee for faculty recruitment rather than leaving the selection to a single hiring officer—but it's useful to determine how broad the disagreement is about these matters early in the process. In this way, people have an opportunity to make their case and perhaps change the minds of others on the committee before the selection process is underway. The best possible result of this discussion is thus not necessarily for everyone to be in absolute agreement about how to rank the various priorities in the search but for there to be at least some general agreement about the three or four items that people regard as most significant.

- The search chair or the administrator who is charging the committee should consider reminding those on the committee not to make assumptions about what a candidate may or may not prefer. It's not uncommon for members of a search committee to say something like, "Oh, we could never meet her salary expectations" or "Why in the world would he want to leave Prestigious International University to come here?" or "We'll never get someone with a doctorate to accept the teaching load assigned to this position." The fact is that candidates make decisions about whether to accept a given job for a variety of reasons. An applicant may be willing to accept a low-paying job or one at a less-well-known institution because he or she has an aging parent in the area, doesn't feel a sense of rapport with his or her current colleagues, wants to be in on the ground floor in building a new program, or any other of a dozen or more reasons. Generally speaking, it's poor practice to exclude any highly qualified candidate from consideration on the basis of an assumption we make on that person's behalf rather than a stated preference or concern by the applicant him- or herself.

• When charging the search committee with its task, it's also a good idea to remind the members to disclose to the committee if they know any of the applicants. Prior knowledge of an applicant is not necessarily a bad thing. It can bring the committee insights that it might not get from the application alone. But it has the potential for being problematic if the member of the search committee has had such a close personal relationship with an applicant that he or she can't be objective about that person. Disclosing prior knowledge of applicants enables the search chair (or someone else whose opinion others will trust) to decide whether that committee member should recuse him- or herself from any decision made about that applicant. It's important that the decision not be left up to the member individually. In the vast majority of cases, the search committee member will truly believe that he or she can be objective about someone who is a close friend, was a former romantic partner, became a fierce intellectual rival, or had some other relationship with the person that could cloud his or her judgment. An impartial opinion about whether the committee member should be disqualified from decisions made about that applicant will lead to a fairer process and decrease the potential for problems down the road. Because committee members don't yet know who's in the applicant pool, they may not be aware that one of these situations exists. For this reason, you may want to urge members of the committee to disclose their relationship with a candidate as soon as possible.

## best practices in screening the applications

It's crucial for search committee chairs to take these steps in providing a clear charge to others because effective screening involves finding a balance between two potential extremes. On the one hand, search committee members need to apply their own expertise, insights, and judgment to the review process. Different members of the committee will bring different perspectives to bear on the review, and what one person might miss another might well catch. On the other hand, if there isn't at least a degree of consistency in how people screen the applications, the group could end up with such divergent views of the applicants that it's all but impossible to decide which of them to advance to the next level of consideration. For this reason, combining a specific charge to the committee with a standardized evaluation form can help provide the right amount of consistency while still enabling committee members to take full advantage of their individual perspectives.

Creating your own standardized screening form for search committees shouldn't involve reinventing the wheel. There are a number of excellent examples developed by colleges and universities, including the following:

- Many institutions have adopted a form that was created as part of the University of Michigan's ADVANCE Program. It appears on page 22 of the *Academic Affairs Hiring Manual* (2015–2016). A few institutions that have either adopted or adapted this form include the University of California at Berkeley (n.d.), the University of Pennsylvania (n.d.), and Harvard University (n.d.).
- The "Faculty Candidate Assessment Form" developed by the University of Florida (n.d.).
- The "Academic Finalist Interview Evaluation Form" developed by San Jose State University (2015).
- Six different forms for evaluating candidates developed by the University of Virginia, Office of University Advancement (n.d.).

In Appendix A, I've included another candidate evaluation form that you can adapt to your specific needs. This sample form combines the best practices found in the forms previously listed and a few other features that may be useful in screening candidates effectively. Although this form is designed to be a universal instrument that can be used for initial screening of applications, telephone interviews, reference checks, finalist interviews, and other reasons, some institutions find it useful to create separate forms for each of these purposes. The result is a series of shorter forms that are more specifically tailored to the needs of different levels of review. Other institutions prefer a single, unified form for the sake of ease and consistency. Either approach can work well, as long as those who complete the forms take them seriously and complete them in a professional manner.

When performing an initial screening of applications, the first criterion, as we've seen, is to distinguished qualified from unqualified applicants. That selection is made on the basis of the criteria that were designated as required in the position announcement or search advertisements. In searches that receive large numbers of applications, the most expedient procedure for committee members to adopt is to perform a quick sort that simply removes the applications of unqualified candidates from the rest of the pool. That process can usually be performed rather rapidly and, by doing so, the person performing the review is then free to devote more time to reviewing the applications of candidates who should receive more complete consideration.

How the committee reports these initial findings to the search chair may be designated by the institution or may simply be up to the discretion of the chair. If the latter is the case, the chair may want to think carefully about the best way in which committee members should organize their findings.

- In relatively small searches, it may be desirable for each committee member to rank the candidates in order of preference. Doing so enables the search chair to determine easily whether a small number of candidates immediately rises to the top of the rankings.
- In larger searches, a strict numerical ranking is time-consuming and probably not particularly helpful. In a search with more than 200 applicants, is it really possible to determine with any accuracy that the candidate ranked 97th is more qualified than the candidate ranked 98th or even 123rd? For this reason, sorting the pool of applicants into such subgroups as unqualified, qualified (those who meet the requirements), and highly competitive (those who meet the requirements and would bring additional attributes and achievements to the position),

or first-tier, second-tier, and third-tier preferences might be a better approach.

- In some cases, it may be desirable to combine these approaches, asking members of the search committee to first sort the applicants into groups by whether they are highly competitive, qualified, or unqualified and then to rank their top three to five most preferred candidates in the highly competitive tier. This approach is time efficient because it doesn't require ranking every applicant and is likely to produce a more productive discussion at a follow-up meeting because committee members will be ready to articulate reasons for preferring that highly select group of applicants.

## ○ best practices for narrowing the pool

Once search committee members have done their initial review of applications, eliminated unqualified candidates, and identified whom they believe to be the strongest candidates, it's time to begin preparing a *short list* of candidates to examine in depth. The size of the short list—and even the number of iterations (i.e., do you start with a short list that you then narrow down to an even shorter list at a subsequent meeting?)— will depend on how many applications you received, how much time you have available for the search, and the level of the position. Most search committees find that a short list of 8 to 20 semifinalists works best. It's focused enough that people can devote sufficient attention to each semifinalist but large enough to provide a diverse pool of candidates with sufficiently varied backgrounds.

The meeting at which the short list of semifinalists is selected is sometimes called a *winnowing meeting*. There's no single right way to conduct a winnowing meeting, but there's one clear wrong way and, unfortunately, it's a procedure that's common at a large number of colleges and universities: The committee discusses each applicant individually and tries to develop a recommendation as to whether that candidate should be made a semifinalist, still kept in consideration in case he or she is needed later, or dropped from consideration entirely. That process is inefficient and ineffective. It's inefficient because the committee ends up spending a great deal of time discussing candidates whom they don't seriously expect to hire or even interview. It's ineffective because committees usually end up spending a lot more time discussing the first few candidates than they do the last few, despite their levels of qualifications. The result is that, if the committee goes through the candidates alphabetically, those applicants whose names begin with letters in the first part of the alphabet are advantaged and those whose names begin with letters in the last part of the alphabet are disadvantaged. If the committee goes through the candidates by their date of application, those who applied early are advantaged, and those who applied late are disadvantaged. Sometimes people try to justify this approach by saying that there should be a reward for early application and a penalty for procrastination. But highly competitive candidates apply late to searches for many valid reasons. They may be trying to keep their interest in other jobs a secret from their employer for as long as possible. They may be waiting on a letter of reference or nomination from a distinguished but very busy mentor. Their research may occupy so much time that they've only just had a chance to submit an application before the deadline. It simply can't be assumed that people apply for jobs near the deadline because they're lazy or uninterested.

---

There are a number of factors that search committees sometimes overlook when seeking to narrow a candidate pool. These are the value-added aspects of a search that may be lost when reviewers focus too exclusively on credentials and scholarly achievements.

- *Mentoring and advising*: Does the applicant provide any evidence of successfully advising or mentoring students?
- *Accreditation*: Does the applicant have any experience dealing with accreditation agencies or participating in successful accreditation efforts?
- *Community relations*: Did the applicant provide evidence of developing and maintaining good relations with businesses or the community?
- *Interpersonal relations*: What can you conclude from the style of the application letter that may provide insight into what it would be like to work with this person as a colleague?

There are two ways of conducting the winnowing meeting that are likely to yield better results. Both require the committee members to have made a serious initial review of the applications before the meeting and to arrive well prepared to discuss individual applications in detail. The first method is to have members of the committee submit their initial reviews of the candidates a day or two before the meeting and then to compile those lists into a single set of rankings. If the charge to the committee was to group the applicants by category (highly competitive, qualified, and unqualified), these lists can easily be generated by assigning points to a candidate on the basis of how he or she is classified by each committee member. There's nothing special about using three tiers for classification other than that most people tend to see candidates as ranking somewhere near the top of the group, in the middle, or at the bottom. Some institutions use as many as five categories in order to develop more nuanced ratings. The one thing that does matter is how you assign points. Candidates in the lowest tier of a committee member's evaluation should receive no points, with each higher category receiving one more point than the category below. A computer spreadsheet can automatically tally these scores and then sort the applicants from highest score to lowest.

When the committee looks at the resulting list, several conclusions are likely. First, there will probably be a group of people at the bottom of the list who either received no points at all or perhaps only a point or two. They can quickly be removed from further consideration. Second, there will often be clear gaps in the scoring at various points. For example, depending on the size of the search committee, there might be a group of candidates with scores above 40, then a gap, and the next cluster of candidates receiving a score no higher than 32 or 33. To make the best use of the committee's time, the chair might suggest that the group initially should focus its attention on the candidates whose scores are above the gap, looking at those with lower scores only if sufficient time remains later in the meeting. In this way, the committee devotes the majority of its time and attention to the applicants who were widely regarded by all the members as the best in the pool.

A similar process can be used if the committee was charged to do their initial screening not by placing applicants into three or more categories but by ranking all the candidates in priority order. If every search committee member has followed instructions and ranked every candidate on a single, continuously numbered list, the candidates can simply be scored by assigning them points according to their place on each member's list. In other words, the top candidate on the list receives 1 point, the 5th candidate receives 5, the 20th candidate receives 20, and so on. Then, when ranking the candidates, instead or listing them as we did by "tennis rules" (in which the highest score wins), you list them by "golf rules" (in which the lowest score wins). In order for this system to work, however, each member of the committee must have ranked all the candidates in a single, continuously numbered list. If even one committee member neglected to rank a candidate, the system won't work properly. Because an unranked candidate receives zero points from that reviewer, that candidate receives an unfair advantage. After all, in golf rules a zero is even better than a one. Similarly, if a reviewer ranks four candidates all as number 5 and seven as number 10 because "they were so equally qualified it was impossible to distinguish them," that reviewer's scores will distort the result. No candidate on his or her list will receive a score as high as some of the applicants on the other reviewers' lists, and so this single reviewer could cause one or more applicants to receive lower (i.e., better) scores and jump ahead of other candidates that the committee as a whole might prefer.

The solution, in this case, is to do one of two things. Either renumber the lists backward or divide each list into thirds or quarters. Renumbering the list backward works like this: Suppose a search has 250 applicants. A candidate who ranks first on a committee member's list receives 250 points, a candidate who ranks second receives 249, and so on. When the scores are tallied, the lists are now sorted by tennis rules with the highest score moving to the top. Because candidates who are unranked on anyone's list receive zero points, they now don't receive an unfair advantage. And because multiple candidates who are given the same ranking receive the same number of points, that reviewer's list ends up assigning fewer total points, which distorts the overall results less.

Dividing each list into thirds or quarters basically converts a ranked list of candidates into a categorized list of candidates similar to the examples we discussed previously. But the important thing to remember is that each reviewer's list should be divided on the basis of its own total number. In other words, suppose a search receives 150 applicants. A reviewer's list that is complete and continuously numbered would then be divided into, say, three groups of 50 (numbers 1–50, 51–100, and 101–150). But if a reviewer's list is incomplete or clusters several applicants with the same ranking, the total number of items in each category should be lower. For example, if a member of the search committee ranks only 120 applicants, you should divide this list into three groups of 40, not two of 50 and one of 20. If you try to include 50 names in the top two tiers for this reviewer, you end up unduly favoring certain applicants and possibly distorting your result.

The second major way of conducting the winnowing meeting doesn't require committee members to submit their rankings in advance. All it requires is for them to order their notes or rankings in the same way, usually alphabetically by the applicant's last name or by his or her date of application. With this approach, the committee chair conducts the meeting by reading each candidate's name at a moderate pace in the same order as the members' notes or rankings. Committee members are instructed to say *yes* if they believe that candidate deserves further consideration and to remain silent if they don't. If even one member of the committee says *yes*, that candidate's materials are set aside for further review. If everyone remains silent, that candidate's materials are eliminated from further consideration. Using this method, it's possible to winnow even a very large pool of candidates into manageable groups of semifinalists in a short amount of time. If, at the end of the process, the pool of semifinalists seems insufficiently diverse or inadequate for any other reason, it's always possible to go back to the full pool and take an additional look at other candidates. But as a quick way of winnowing very large lists of candidates, this simple approach is surprisingly effective.

Red flags to watch out for when reviewing applications:

- The candidate not holding positions very long
- Inexplicable gaps in a candidate's history
- Overt contempt or lack of respect for a current or previous institution
- Evidence of conflict (even personality conflict) with more than one supervisor or colleague
- Your own tendency to fixate on a single attribute or qualification (Remember to review applications holistically. Don't overuse litmus test items.)

## ° best practices in reducing the short list

Even though the search committee will cut the full list of applicants to a short list of those who are highly competitive, it's almost certain that the resulting list will still be too long for on-campus interviews to be granted to everyone it includes. For this reason, the short list needs to be winnowed even further to a very small list of finalists. The number of finalists you choose will depend on your institution, its past practices, and the type of position you have available. Many people assume that the more senior or prestigious the position, the more finalists a search committee will want to include. In fact, the opposite is often the case. For distinguished senior professor positions, you may discover than only one or two applicants in the entire pool clearly have the superior level of qualifications you're looking for. In searches for entry-level positions, however, there may be a fairly large number of candidates who all appear to have qualifications and attributes that can benefit your program. So, despite what some people may claim is the rule for the number of finalists in a national search for a faculty member, there really are no hard and fast principles unless the institution itself requires that a minimum number of candidates be interviewed. Nevertheless, the following *guidelines* may be considered best practices in faculty recruitment:

- It is common for colleges and universities to bring in three or four finalists for most full-time faculty positions. This number is large enough to increase the likelihood that the finalist pool will contain sufficient diversity but not so large that people will start forgetting about the first candidate by the time they meet the last.

- In times of fiscal constraint, some colleges and universities adopt a practice of bringing in two candidates and then proceeding to a third candidate only if there's not a clear desire to hire one of the first two. This practice is certainly acceptable as long as it isn't used as a ploy to decrease the diversity of the finalist pool.

- Occasionally a pool will be so weak that there is only one clearly competitive candidate remaining after narrowing the short list. A dilemma then results: Should the deadline be extended at the risk that the remaining semifinalist will find a job elsewhere or should that candidate be interviewed now at the risk that a decision will be made on the basis of personal contact with only one applicant? In this situation, no hard and fast rule can be given. If the original deadline was still early in the recruitment season, it may be best to extend the deadline. But if it's already late in the search season, the candidate is so truly phenomenal that he or she is unlikely to remain on the market very long, or the candidate would help the program achieve an important goal (such as diversifying the faculty or bringing significant grant funding to the institution), it may be best to interview that candidate and then decide to extend the search if things don't work out. For this reason, every possible consideration needs to be made by the search committee, chair, and dean before a well-informed decision can be made. Fortunately these situations are relatively rare.

- Only in extremely unusual circumstances should more than three finalists be brought in for interviews for reasons that we'll consider in the following discussion.

While search committees are reducing the short list to a set of finalists who will be interviewed on campus, a phenomenon tends to occur that's so familiar to deans and department chairs that I call it *what every search committee will tell you* (or *WESCWTY*). Here's how WESCWTY works. One day the chair of the search committee comes to the office of whoever's ultimately in charge of hiring the faculty member and says,

"Look, I know we're only supposed to bring three candidates to campus. But Candidate X lives locally [or perhaps is an internal candidate], and so it won't cost us that much more to invite in *four* candidates. So, can we get permission to have four on-campus interviews?" On its surface the request seems logical enough. More choice is often better. And if you can have more choice without adding cost to the process, why not go ahead and do so? The answer is that adding extra finalists to an interview process has far more drawbacks than advantages, and ultimately the search committee may well regret that you yielded to this seemingly reasonable request. Here's why.

WESCWTY is always presented as being either cost neutral or requiring a very minor additional investment on the part of the institution. But what those who make this suggestion often don't realize until interviews are well underway is that money isn't the only resource involved in a search. A properly conducted interview also requires extensive investments of time and energy. Candidates have to be escorted from one meeting to the next, entertained, fed, questioned, and evaluated. If the chair of the search committee points this out to the group, the objection may be made that, because the candidate is local or already an employee, these considerations don't apply. There will be no drive from the airport, no need to take the person to another building that he or she already knows well, and no need to provide special meals. But conducting a search that way poses problems. As described in Chapter 4 when we consider special considerations to keep in mind when dealing with internal candidates or incumbents, the more differences we make in the schedule of any one candidate, the more atypical his or her experience becomes relative to that of the other applicants.

Search committee members gain valuable insights as they walk across campus with a candidate (even if that candidate is already well known to them) or share a meal. If you don't provide equivalent experiences for every candidate, you open the door to an accusation of unfairness no matter what the decision is. If the local candidate gets the job after a scaled-down search process, it looks to the other candidates as though the process was fixed in favor of the candidate who was hired. If the local candidate isn't chosen, then he or she is likely to complain that the other candidates had more time with the search committee. Members of the search committee may ask you how other candidates can possibly find out about the internal candidate's experience once they leave campus. The answer is that we live in a small, interconnected world and, regardless of how the other candidates learn these things, they inevitably do.

In addition, properly conducted searches are exhausting. The same search committee that begs for four candidates to be interviewed early in the process will often wish later that the process could be completed after meeting only one or two. Those involved in interviews discover that courses have to be rescheduled in order to clear the day for meeting with the candidates and attending public presentations. Faculty members have to devote evenings to meals with that day's finalist or trips to the airport or hotel. (At some schools, the members of the search committee even have to pay for their own meals when dining off campus with a candidate.) Follow-up calls will sometimes have to be made in order to gain more information after a candidate's departure. Chairs and deans will have to block out time in their day, even if they are only having courtesy calls with each candidate. In short, gearing up for an on-campus interview drains the energy of everyone involved. If you do conduct more interviews than necessary to make the search thorough and fair, you'll have far less energy to devote to all the other activities central to a faculty position—such as teaching your courses and conducting your research.

Another major reason why expanding the interview pool is expensive has to do with the cost an extended process has on the search's fairness to all candidates. In any series of interviews, the person who goes first may well be at a disadvantage. Even if the interviews all take place on successive days, memories of a candidate become surprisingly hazy once the search committee and other interviewers have spoken to one or two more people. Moreover, search committees sharpen their skills over the course of an interview process. By the time they meet with the third candidate, they know what questions they really need to ask and how best to phrase each question. The committee members may unconsciously hold it against an early candidate that he or she didn't happen address a specific issue, even though they didn't think of asking about it until later in the process. That situation, which is true in all searches, can become even more exacerbated as the number of interviewees expands. So, by adding an additional applicant to the finalist list, you are creating a genuine disadvantage for the first candidate and may end up treating that person unfairly.

But perhaps the most important reason why administrators turn down a request to interview additional candidates is that a prolonged process alleviates the search committee's need to screen the applicants as thoroughly as they should. Consciously or not, people may be tempted to offer a courtesy interview to an internal or local candidate merely because it seems the polite thing to do. But, as described in Chapter 4, interviewing a candidate who's not as competitive as the others is always a mistake. It raises that candidate's expectations and, if he or she later discovers that the committee was basically just going through the motions of an interview, the candidate may well be even more upset than if no interview was offered in the first place. In certain instances, the result may be a grievance or lawsuit. For this reason, by forcing the committee to limit its interviews to the three *best* candidates, regardless of their location, those who are conducting the search will be compelled to focus their attention on the applicants who are most qualified and likely to be offered the job.

WESCWTY is often presented to those in charge of searches as though it is a creative and original idea. It isn't. It's a request that is regarded as an effective solution even though, as we've just seen, there are compelling reasons why it's a bad idea. So, if your fellow members on the search committee still don't believe you after outlining these arguments, show them this chapter. At the very least, it will be proof that their "original idea" isn't all that original.

## o   best practices for making reference calls

Calls to a candidate's references can be particularly effective at two points in the search process: when narrowing the short list to finalists and when on-campus interviews are over and one applicant must be selected and hired. These two types of reference calls serve different purposes. Those conducted before the on-campus interviews help the search committee learn more about the applicant as a real person and see beyond what can be learned from the paperwork he or she has submitted. Those conducted after interviews are over can help clarify any impressions of the candidate about which the search committee is in doubt, validate statements he or she made in the interview, and send an indirect message to the candidate that he or she is being considered very seriously for the position. That last point falls more into the category of recruitment strategy and may require some clarification. When references are contacted, they almost always notify the applicant that they received a call. Even if you ask references not to do so, they probably will. It's human nature. References tend to be the candidate's mentors or otherwise very close to the candidate; they want to pass on the good news that an institution is giving them serious consideration for the job. Frequently when we interview candidates, particularly for senior positions or those that are difficult to fill, we become concerned that another school will hire our best applicant before we can get an offer ready. By spacing out reference calls to fill the gap between the interview and the offer, we can send a subtle message to the candidate that his or her application is still viable and that we're still very much interested in the possibility of hiring him or her.

Regardless of whether reference calls are made before or after the interview, there are several best practices to keep in mind:

- Be respectful of the person's time. References are frequently senior professors or administrators. Your reference call about this candidate is unlikely to be the only one the person receives. Asking the person to take a half-hour or more out of a busy day to speak to the search committee simply wastes the person's time and makes your search effort look unprofessional. Ten minutes should be the maximum amount of time you ask a reference to devote to a call; 5 minutes is even better.
- Be well prepared for the call. Have your questions prepared in advance and know exactly what you want to ask. You're likely to be

prepared in this way when you initially make the call. But, because references are usually very busy people, you may well have to leave a message to have the person call you back. (In light of the previous point, you may want to stress in your message how brief the return call needs to be. If you say something such as "I just need 45 minutes or an hour of your time," you drastically decrease the likelihood that you'll receive a return call.) For this reason, you'll need to be constantly prepared for the call regardless of when the reference contacts you. Keep your list of questions next to the phone on which the person will reach you or store them on an electronic device you'll always have available. If the person will call you on your cell phone, you don't want the list stored there, of course; you won't be able to see the list and talk to the person (at least not easily) at the same time.

- Ask questions that only the reference can answer for you. Don't ask about anything you could learn from the candidate's application, résumé, website, or other sources. Questions about collegiality and teamwork are particularly good for references. But remember that a question such as "Is this person collegial?" won't tell you what you need to know. If the reference wants the candidate to be hired, there's only one way to answer this question. Better ways of addressing this issue include asking for an example of how this person remained collegial in a challenging situation, asking about an incident in which this person demonstrated that she or he truly believed in teamwork, and asking how this person responds when angry or frustrated. Ask about the quality of the candidate's research only if the reference is in a better position to evaluate it than anyone involved in the search at your institution. Always remember to close by asking, "Do you know anything about this person that, if I knew it, might make me hesitate to hire him or her?" The only correct answer to this question is an immediate, emphatic *no*. If the reference even pauses a moment to think about how to respond, that answer is a red flag that you should take very seriously.

There are a number of things you can learn from reference calls that you might not find out any other way. Consider asking each reference about these aspects of the candidate:

- Level of confidence
- Level of enthusiasm
- Reliability
- Energy level
- Degree of talkativeness
- Tendency to gossip
- Ability to handle criticism
- Ability to cope with change
- Detail orientation versus big-picture orientation

## ○ best practices in conducting phone or video interviews

The most common way of reducing the short list to a small group of finalists who can be brought to campus for interviews is to conduct a prescreening interview by phone or videoconference. For very high-level faculty positions, some institutions may conduct airport interviews, those medium-length interviews typically conducted either in an airport conference room or a nearby hotel. The advantage of this approach is that it's possible to interview everyone on the short list in only a day or two. But airport interviews are expensive because it involves flying 10 or more candidates to a central location, with many of them flying back home the same day. And so, airport interviews are quite uncommon in faculty searches. Other ways of screening the candidates have to be found.

For many years, the most common method that was used to reduce the short list of candidates was a telephone interview with a member of the search committee or a conference call with several (or perhaps all) of the members. More recently, videoconferencing either through special videoconference rooms or by means of personal videoconference software (such as Facetime and Skype) has become a useful alternative to traditional phone interviews. But there's a key principle to keep in mind when deciding which of these approaches to use.

> Interview each semifinalist the same way.

If you conduct some interviews by telephone and others by video, you end up with experiences that can't properly be compared. In video interviews, you learn certain things that you won't know about the candidates you spoke to by telephone. For example, a person's expression might brighten while speaking about a current student in a way that doesn't come through in that person's voice alone. Conversely, the candidates also gain certain information about you in a video interview. The facial expression you unintentionally adopt, even for a split second, when someone gives a very good or unbelievably bad answer isn't available to someone on the phone. The candidate in the video conference might then elaborate an answer that seemed to interest you or salvage an answer that concerned you because of insight that candidates on the phone don't receive. But those semifinalists who are speaking to you on the phone have advantages that the video candidates don't have. They can spread out sheets of paper with facts, figures, and talking points all around them and thus come across as far more knowledgeable than a candidate on camera who doesn't have the luxury of referring to notes. In short, a phone call is a different experience from a videoconference. So, if you want to make meaningful comparisons and contrasts, provide each semifinalist with the same experience.

Appendix A provides a candidate rating form that interviewers can use to ensure greater consistency in evaluation. In Appendix B, you'll find some useful questions to ask the candidates. In general, good screening questions at this point in the search involve follow-up on any item that seemed unclear in the candidate's materials, issues that give you a sense of the candidate's priorities and career trajectory (in order for you to determine which semifinalists seem best suited for your institution and program), and matters that give you a sense of the candidate as a person. Unless a résumé seems out of date, it's a poor practice to waste valuable interview time asking someone about the number of articles he or she has written (you can count them) or where he or she received various degrees (you can read that for yourself). Instead choose each question with the following goal in mind: What will tell me whether I'd like to have this person working alongside me as a colleague, contributing to the success of our program, and making us even better than we already are?

## ○ best practices for achieving consensus on finalists

In many searches, the review of application materials and conversations with references and the candidates themselves will make it readily apparent to members of the committee who the most competitive candidates are. In some cases, however, that choice may not be as clear-cut. Either there won't be any consensus at all as to who the finalists should be or a clear consensus will emerge for one or two candidates but not for as many finalists as the institution typically interviews. As an initial step in this selection process, therefore, it's usually helpful for the committee members to rank in order of preference a slightly greater number of candidates than it actually tends to interview. For example, if three finalists will be interviewed, committee members might each rank their top five candidates. At this stage in the search, because only a limited number of finalists can be brought in for interviews, the search chair can insist that all members of the committee rank five and only five candidates and that each list be in continuous order without ties. If a committee member refuses to do so and submits a list of 10 names, only the first five will be considered. If someone submits a list with three people tied for second place, that list will be returned to the committee member to be redone until the person provides a single continuous ranking. If after repeated requests the committee member says that he or she cannot make a choice among equally qualified candidates, the search chair should remind the committee member that the group will *have* to make a choice because only one applicant can be hired for the position. If after repeated requests, the search committee member still does not comply, then set that ballot aside, and base a finalist ranking only on the lists provided by the committee members who properly followed directions.

If this procedure is followed, the chair can then adopt the golf rules approach for tallying the ballots: The candidates with the lowest scores win. Before making a final decision, however, the search chair should meet with the committee, explain how the finalists were selected, and ask the group if the choices emerging from this process are satisfactory to everyone. Doing so allows a committee member who feels strongly about a candidate whose name doesn't appear among the finalists to make the case that the candidate deserves another look. Following this discussion, a vote should be taken and recorded to reflect that the group of finalists truly reflects the best judgment of the committee. In addition to the finalists, a group of alternates should also be ranked. One or more of the finalists may no longer be available for an on-campus interview or, after those interviews, none of the remaining candidates who are acceptable may agree to take the job. Having this kind of back-up plan enables the committee to proceed quickly to alternates when the need arises. And that need does arise in a significant number of searches.

> Never include any candidate on an alternate list who isn't truly viable. It's always better to abort a search, extend it, or hire someone on a short-term contract than to hire a less-than-desirable candidate on a tenure-track or multiyear contract.

If the committee finds that it simply can't agree on who the finalists for a search should be, that's a sign that the group isn't yet ready to make that choice. Perhaps the position hasn't been defined clearly enough or the charge to the committee didn't provide sufficient guidance. Whatever the reason, the best practice is not to force a choice of finalists that only one or two members of the group support and the others grudgingly accept. It's better to take a step back, reconsider the goals the program has for this particular position, and take a fresh look at the entire applicant pool. In most cases, that discussion can't begin for at least a few days after the deadlock was reached so that any residual frustration or anger arising from the previous discussion can subside. Allowing a bit of a break between discussions will enable the group to return to its deliberations with new energy and fresh eyes.

## ○ putting it all together

Although the winnowing meetings at which semifinalists and finalists are selected may be laborious and time-consuming, they're probably the single most important part of the search. Selecting the one person who will be hired from among the candidates usually involves choosing from among several highly competitive, fully qualified candidates. In many cases, the program will be well served regardless of which finalist is hired. But the prior stage in the selection process involves distinguishing qualified from unqualified candidates, highly competitive from competitive candidates, and excellent choices from merely good choices. Because it involves identifying the small pool from which a future colleague will be chosen, it is a critically important step in the search process and needs to be approached with care, attention to detail, and the ability to see the big picture. It's not always easy to find search committee members who possess all those traits simultaneously—while still having a committee that reflects a desirable level of diversity and professional expertise in the appropriate subject area—but the right mix is critical for the program to flourish.

Perhaps the most important factor in a successful review of applications is the charge that the dean, department chair, or committee chair gives the others in the group. Without clear guidance, some committee members will simply give preference to people who are just like them or who will help them advance a cause that, although important to them, isn't a key factor in the current search. Well-designed candidate evaluation forms (see Appendix A) are helpful, but the chair's instructions and ability to outline clear priorities are indispensable. For this reason, search chairs should be, whenever possible, people who are experienced in previous searches at your institution, have good people skills (including the ability to mediate disagreements and build consensus), and possess the ability to look beyond personal interests to what is most needed for the program and institution to be successful.

# 4

# scheduling the interviews

At many institutions, the process of scheduling candidate interviews involves little more than taking the agenda used during a previous interview and updating it with different names. But if we want to improve our chance of hiring the right candidate, we need to ask the question, Is what we've always been doing in previous interviews the best way to give us the insights we really need into each candidate's strengths and weaknesses? In order to answer this question, we'll begin with a short thought experiment.

Imagine that a friend of yours is getting married. She wants to choose a baker for her wedding cake and has a choice:

- She can have each baker send her cake samples to taste.
- She can meet with each baker and have the baker talk with her about the process of baking.

Which approach do you recommend that she take?

Most people will find the choice rather obvious. She'd learn much more if she actually sampled the baker's wares than if they merely had a conversation about baking. And yet most interview processes in higher education are little more than the academic equivalent of merely talking about the process of baking. We schedule meeting after meeting in which various stakeholders ask the candidate questions about teaching, research, and service rather than actually observing the candidate teach, perform research, and serve. Moreover, the questions each stakeholder asks are often very much the same as those the last stakeholder asked, and so the candidate is put through a wearying process of saying the same thing over and over while showing us very little of what he or she can actually do.

Moreover, decades of research have repeatedly demonstrated that traditional interviews are notoriously imperfect ways of predicting which candidates will succeed in a job (see, for example, Conway, Jako, & Goodman, 1995; Hosoda, Stone-Romero, & Coats, 2003; McDaniel, Whetzel, Schmidt, & Maurer, 1994; Schmidt & Hunter, 1998).

> Anyone can fake it for at least a day or two and seem to be the sort of person you'd want to hire.

The typical academic interview only lasts for a day or two. Some are even shorter. That's unlikely to be long enough to see the person behind the façade. In the words of the human resources specialist John Sullivan:

> **Interviews are inherently misleading**—the basic foundation of the interview is based on the premise that during the interview, candidates are acting normally and are telling the truth. This is unlikely because most candidates are scared to death before, during, and after interviews. The interview situation is by definition "unreal" and words often should not be taken as proof. It is not "the job" and therefore what happens during the interview might not be representative of what one would actually do on the job. . . . [I]nterviewees frequently provide the answers that they believe that the interviewer wants to hear, rather than the most accurate answer. Interviewees frequently lie or omit key facts; unfortunately, interviewers do the same. (Sullivan, 2012)

The solution to this problem is to reexamine how we design and schedule academic job interviews. Rather than assuming an interview has to be a series of question-and-answer sessions, it's possible to construct them quite differently.

> Think of the interview process as a kind of audition. Candidates shouldn't just *tell* you what they can do. They should also *show* you.

The result is a process known as *performance-based interviewing* and through it we learn far more about candidates than we do using the outdated system still in use at most colleges and universities. Performance-based interviewing begins with identifying your unmet program needs and focuses on two primary questions:

- What will the person we hire actually be doing in this job?
- What are the best ways we have of determining whether he or she can do it?

In one of the programs where I worked, we were consistently hiring administrative assistants who simply weren't capable of doing the job. As we examined our hiring process, it quickly became apparent why this was the case: We were *asking* candidates about their skills rather than having the candidates *demonstrate* them. Once we implemented a skills test in which each person we interviewed actually had to create a word-processing document, spreadsheet, and other items to certain specifications, it soon became apparent that many candidates overestimated their abilities. Several applicants whom we would've hired because they had excellent interview skills quickly demonstrated that they didn't have equivalent job-related skills. And what works with hiring staff can, with appropriate modifications, be modified to work with hiring faculty members as well.

What might you decide faculty members need to do in order to be successful? Your list might look something like the following:

- Teach a large lecture section of Introduction to Obscurity Studies.
- Teach an online course that receives general education credit such as Obscure Literature: Appreciation and Analysis.
- Teach a medium-sized (30- to 60-student) section of the upper-division undergraduate course Research Methods in Obscurity Studies.
- Teach a seminar-style graduate course such as Current Issues in Obscurity Studies or Incomprehensibility Theory and Practice.
- Make conference presentations to the International League of Obscurity Studies and Obscure Scholars.
- Receive a research grant of more than $5 million every 3 to 6 years.
- Have a book of research closely related to our discipline accepted by a major university press before the sixth-year tenure review.
- Serve on at least one university-wide and two departmental committees before the sixth-year tenure review.
- Maintain collegial and supportive relationships with the other members of the department.
- Help the department build bridges to the School of Hard Knocks and the College of Musical Knowledge.

That's a pretty extensive list, and your first task should be to ask whether every item on it is absolutely necessary. In developing a list of abilities to look for in a performance-based interview, you may need to refine an initially massive list of wants into a more manageable list of genuine needs. For example, if the candidate turns out not to be very good at large lecture classes but satisfies all the rest of the criteria on the list, would you really feel that he or she has not been successful? Or what about a faculty member who meets all the other criteria but is a rude and ill-tempered colleague? Would you still feel that he or she has failed in the job? Different institutions—even different departments at the same institution—may answer these questions otherwise, so don't assume that each question has only one right answer.

Once you have focused your list on the most important abilities, skills, and attributes needed to succeed in the job, the next step is to determine the best ways to discover whether each finalist can meet those expectations. And you may well find that the best way *never* turns out to be just asking a lot of questions in a traditional interview. Instead, you may think of ideas such as the following:

- Set up a laptop with a video camera and live-streaming software in several courses that the candidate is currently teaching at his or her present institution. Observe how the candidate presents information, interacts with students, structures lessons, and so on.
- Involve the candidate in a brief role-playing scenario in which he or she has to deal with some of the challenges faculty members face daily at your institution.
- Have the candidate present a mock session of an online course with the search committee as students.
- Arrange for the candidate to serve as a guest instructor for half an hour in three courses that enroll widely different groups of students: nonmajors taking the course to fulfill a general education requirement, upper division majors, and doctoral students in the discipline.
- When asking questions of the candidate, include a number of hypothetical situations and ask how he or she might deal with each situation.
- Ask the applicant to review the program's current curriculum and course rotation and make recommendations on how it could be improved.
- Have each candidate meet with a student who is conducting research in the discipline and critique his or her thesis chapter or project.
- Invite the candidate to attend a committee meeting in the department and make a few suggestions about whatever issue is being discussed.
- Structure the candidate's job talk so that it parallels the format used for presentations at the national conference in the discipline and ask the type of questions typically generated at these meetings.

- Ask the candidate to review two grant applications recently submitted by the department, one of which was funded and the other of which was rejected, and offer reactions and suggestions.
- In addition to submitting one or two examples of published work, require the candidate to submit the current draft of a research publication that is still in progress.

Just as with your list of what a faculty member will need to do in order to succeed at your institution, these performance-based interview approaches are likely to need editing once they're conceived. After all, neither the search committee nor the candidates will have enough time for all the activities you come up with. But even with a far shorter set of performance-based activities, you're likely to learn far more about each candidate than you would from a traditional interview. (For more on performance-based interviewing, see Hochel & Wilson, 2007, pp. 80–83.)

You can free up more time in the interview schedule by eliminating meetings at which the candidate answers questions posed by different groups and combining all question-and-answer sessions into a single meeting that all stakeholders may attend. In this way, everyone will hear the same thing, and there will be less likelihood of one group getting one answer because of how the question is posed while another group getting what it believes to be a completely different answer because it phrased its question differently. Some search committee members may be reluctant to adopt this single-question-session approach because they feel that students may be reluctant to ask questions when faculty members are present, faculty members may be reluctant to ask questions when the department chair and dean are present, and so on. In actual practice, this fear rarely tends to be well-founded. A skilled facilitator can prompt questions by saying things such as "We haven't heard from any of the undergraduates yet. Is there a student who has a question?" or "I know that some of our junior faculty may have a few questions because they've recently been through this same process. Which of our recent hires might like to pose a question?" These single-question-sessions are usually best when they're held near the end of the interview process. By that time, people will have observed the candidate in action as he or she taught courses, gave research presentations, and engaged in other performance-based activities. The questions will be better focused because they will have been shaped by more thorough knowledge of the applicant than can occur by reading a résumé alone.

> When you schedule question-and-answer sessions near the end of an interview process rather than at the beginning, you know better what to ask because of what you've observed the candidate doing for the past day or so.

## ○  scheduling comparable interview processes

In scheduling candidate interviews, best practices dictate that the process for each candidate should be as similar as possible to that of any other candidate. There are several reasons for this practice. First, it's a matter of fairness to the candidates. If one applicant is given an opportunity to use the latest technology while making a presentation and the other applicants speak in a hall with poor acoustics, no projectors, and a sound system that repeatedly squeals with feedback, the first candidate receives an unfair advantage. Second, it's a matter of comparing apples to apples. If one candidate gives a 40-minute research presentation, a second candidate distributes printed copies of the presentation, and a third merely submits the PowerPoint slides that would've been used in a presentation, it's much harder to identify meaningful similarities and contrasts than if all the applicants had done the same thing.

But as important as it is to treat all the candidates fairly and establish a realistic baseline for comparison, it's also important to recognize that *comparable* doesn't mean the same thing as *identical*. Particularly when you're trying to implement your strategy for diversifying the faculty, you may discover that what's appropriate for one candidate isn't really suitable for others. An African American candidate may find it beneficial to meet with the institution's faculty Black caucus, a female candidate might want to speak with the university's forum on women's leadership, and so on. At the same time, you also don't want to assume that those meetings are desired by the candidate and thus leave the candidate thinking, "Oh, I see how people operate here. They assume that, just because I'm Black (or a woman or physically challenged or a member of a religious minority or whatever else might be distinctive), I must have an interest in such-and-such a group. They're still not seeing me as an individual." If that's the image you convey, your efforts to create a positive impression on the candidate will backfire. One practice that some institutions find useful is to send each candidate a list of certain campus groups and local organizations before he or she arrives for a campus interview. The candidate is then told that there will be time built into the schedule to meet with two or three of the groups on the list, *if the candidate chooses to do so.* In this way, it's left to the candidate to decide whether he or she would find certain meetings useful. The search committee doesn't have to try to guess what any particular candidate might prefer.

## ○ searches with incumbents or internal candidates

One situation in which the importance of comparable interview processes proves special importance is when a search involves incumbents or internal candidates. An *incumbent* is someone who currently occupies the position for which you are searching and who will be replaced by the person you hire. An *internal candidate* is an applicant who is already employed by the institution but in a different capacity. Both of these situations require special attention to make sure that the process is as fair as possible for everyone concerned.

### Special Procedures Involving Incumbents

Institutions conduct searches on faculty lines that are already occupied for many reasons. Perhaps the person is retiring or has already accepted but not yet assumed another position. Perhaps the person was terminated or had a contract that was not renewed but his or her final date of employment hasn't yet arrived. Perhaps the person is being reassigned, either willingly or not, to other duties within the institution.

Regardless of the reason for conducting a search for a position that isn't yet vacant, every institution should adhere to one fundamental principle: No incumbent should play any role whatsoever in the search, including being present for interviews or any meetings in which the job description is developed or candidates are discussed.

Although most institutions will regard the principle of excluding incumbents from the search process as simple common sense, others may dismiss it as excessively harsh, even counterintuitive. After all, why would you want to exclude from the search the very person who knows the job best? Can't the incumbent provide valuable information about how the advertisement should be written, how it should be distributed, and whether individual applicants are truly qualified? What harm can it do to have a candidate meet the incumbent, at least socially, and gain a better sense of what the job entails? It's perhaps easiest to begin answering these questions by addressing the last issue first: Involving an incumbent in a search, even tangentially, can do an incredible amount of harm, and many search processes have been corrupted (sometimes intentionally, sometimes accidentally) because an incumbent was not sufficiently quarantined from hiring discussions.

Why is it necessary to keep incumbents removed from the search for their replacements? To begin with, doing so sends a clear message that the position belongs to the *institution,* not to the *person* who holds it. Although employees who have contributed many years of meritorious service to a college or university may initially be hurt to discover that their advice is not being solicited about the choice of their successor, this policy can be easily explained to the incumbent. Simply note that every vacancy provides an opportunity for an institution. Taking full advantage of that opportunity becomes far more difficult when the current occupant of a position is present for those discussions, even if that person is dearly loved and universally admired. We owe it to each finalist for a position to make up his or her own mind about the best direction to take in that job and whether or not the institution is a good fit for that person's immediate needs and long-term goals. It does a disservice to candidates to have their perspectives colored before they have their own chance to decide these matters. Moreover, when incumbents are being relieved of their positions unwillingly, no one would consider permitting a process to become poisoned through a negative or misleading remark. That same strategy must be followed even when the incumbent is vacating the position on the happiest of terms in order to prevent even the slightest impression that the incumbent has had undue influence on the outcome of a search.

> No one in academic life should have a voice in choosing his or her own successor.

If this policy is followed in all cases, then no one will ever need to make those (sometimes very subjective) judgments about whether an incumbent is leaving the institution on good terms or bad. The only thing one needs to do is point to the existence of this rule and explain that, regrettably, exceptions cannot be made.

## Special Procedures Involving Internal Candidates

A different set of issues may arise when an internal candidate applies for a position. In these cases, a current employee wants to be offered the new position, but it's important that he or she not have an unfair advantage over external applicants. Moreover, it is important that other applicants not *even receive the impression* that an internal candidate has had an unfair advantage. If the search proves to be very contentious, an applicant who believes that a search was improperly conducted may file a lawsuit or a complaint with the Equal Opportunity Commission against the school, alleging unfair labor practices. Even in searches where this outcome seems unlikely, external applicants may emerge from the process with hard feelings toward the college or university; if the person then shares those sentiments with others, there could be very undesirable consequences with potential students or donors, and the impact may be far greater than on the search alone. The goal, therefore, must be for *all* candidates to be treated honestly throughout the search, and that goal is more easily achieved if colleges and universities adhere to the following guidelines:

### Never extend an internal candidate a courtesy interview

Some people believe that, because internal candidates are already employees, they should be interviewed even when they are not strong contenders for the position. The assumption seems to be that this type of courtesy interview will make internal applicants feel better about themselves or protect their self-esteem against the stigma of being screened out early in the process. But this type of courtesy interview frequently backfires. It gives the internal applicant the false impression that he or she has a better chance of being offered the position than is actually the case, and it may make external applicants believe that the institution is not conducting an open search. Although it can be awkward to inform an internal candidate early in the process that he or she will not be advanced any further in the search, having that conversation is far preferable to the alternative when internal and external candidates are misled about the integrity of the search.

### When internal candidates are granted interviews, they should be interviewed *before* external candidates

Throughout any search, even privileged information tends to leak. People hear which questions candidates are asked repeatedly, which concerns tend to arise, and the responses (good and bad) of previous applicants. Because it is not proper for an internal candidate to benefit from this knowledge, it is simply good practice to interview all internal candidates before external candidates start arriving on campus.

**Internal candidates should have an experience as close as possible to that of all other candidates**

It can be tempting, because an internal candidate lives in the area, to speak to this applicant in person even though other candidates must be reached by phone or to extend that person's interview process over an entire week, even though other candidates spend only a day or two on campus. These changes make the experience of the internal candidate substantively different from that of all other candidates. In person, the internal candidate may pick up on visual cues, such as an expression of doubt or a frown of disapproval, that other applicants cannot see when they communicate by telephone. When called in their offices, external candidates may, as we've seen, surround themselves with notes or discreetly check a fact on the Internet, an opportunity that is not open to an internal candidate who is interviewed in person. Moreover, internal candidates may be put at a disadvantage if they have to sustain their energy for an extended period of interviews that other candidates were able to complete in a shorter period of time. So, in order to be fair to all applicants, it is important to conduct the process in the same way regardless of whether a candidate lives nearby or must travel a great distance.

**Once an internal candidate has completed an interview, he or she should not be involved in the search process in any other way**

Although it may seem obvious that an internal candidate would not participate in evaluating other applicants for the position, some search committees see no harm in permitting internal candidates to participate in social events where another applicant is present. The problem with this practice is that an external candidate who learns a rival candidate is in the room may be made uncomfortable enough that it affects the outcome of the search. It is often challenging to relax enough to be yourself in any search, but doing so can become all but impossible when you feel your every move is being critiqued by another candidate. Moreover, if the external candidate later withdraws from the search for any reason, you'll never know for certain that the real issue was not an unfortunate remark that the internal candidate made in even the most innocuous social setting. In order to avoid any doubt about the integrity of the search, it is highly desirable to limit the role of all internal candidates to that of being applicants only.

## ○ involving realtors in the interview process

One activity that many institutions include when scheduling interviews is to include a block of time for finalists to tour the community with a realtor. This practice serves many purposes simultaneously. First, it gives candidates a sense of the area and a chance to determine whether they can visualize themselves and their families building a life there. Second, it provides some down time for candidates when they don't feel as though they're under constant scrutiny. Third, it provides a break for the search committee as well because they have plenty of other responsibilities that they can't put on hold entirely throughout the interview process. Fourth, it offers candidates an external perspective on the institution that they may not get otherwise: how it's perceived by members of the community, whether there have been any town-versus-gown conflicts, and so on. Fifth, the candidates receive valuable information about the cost of living in the area and perhaps even form an initial notion of where they might live if offered the job. Sixth, it builds community support because the realtor is likely to make a sale from participating in the search and thus have direct financial reasons for viewing the college or university in a positive light.

But although many institutions schedule candidate tours with realtors for all of these reasons, some of them fail to take advantage of another important contribution this activity can make to the search process: They don't follow up with the realtors about their impressions of the candidates. One of the reasons for not doing so is our tendency in higher education to focus on résumés, credentials, degrees, and publications. If all you're interested in is academic credentials, you're not likely to believe that a realtor (who probably doesn't have an advanced degree) will have useful insight to provide the committee. But search committees forget that, although they're seeing candidates as potential coworkers, realtors are experiencing them just as people. And as we've seen, it's those people skills and attitudes that cause faculty members to fail once they're hired far more often than problems with their academic credentials. Even though candidates don't *feel* as though they're under constant scrutiny when they're out on a realtor's tour, that doesn't mean that the realtor isn't sizing them up. After all, that's part of what realtors do for a living: gain a sense of their clients' desires and needs, how ready they are to make a purchase, and what they're like when they're not selling themselves but rather seeing themselves as potential purchasers. If candidates speak slightingly of the institution or certain members of the faculty and staff when they don't think "anyone important" is listening, that's valuable information for you to have before your hiring decision. If candidates are rude or arrogant when they feel they have impunity, it's useful for you to know that, too.

> There's an old principle that applies to going out on a first date with someone: Pay attention to how your date treats the waitstaff at dinner because, within 6 months, that's how he or she is going to be treating you.
>
> The search committee equivalent of this principle might be similar: Pay attention to what a realtor tells you about a candidate's interactions with people who "don't matter," because, if this person ever gets tenure, that's how he or she is going to be treating you.

What should you do about tours with a realtor if the applicant is an internal candidate? This situation is a good example of how interview processes should be comparable, not necessarily identical. Offer the tour to the internal candidate as an option. It could well be that the person is thinking about moving to a new home if he or she gets the job, or it could be that he or she just wants the same experience the other finalists have. But don't insist on it. If an internal candidate knows the area well enough that he or she thinks such a visit would be a waste of time, honor that decision. The candidate wouldn't gain much from the experience, and there will be other opportunities for the search committee to gain the types of insight that a realtor could provide about that candidate. Members of the search committee may know the person already. If not, there are certainly others at the institution who do, and their impressions can make up for what the realtor would have told you.

## ○ the role of free time in the interview process

A well-designed interview schedule should be a balance between a sufficient number of activities to learn what you need to know about each finalist and a sufficient amount of free time to prevent the candidate from being exhausted. If you don't schedule enough meetings and appointments, some candidates may feel that you're not really interested in them. If you schedule too many, you could end up alienating your finalists by making them feel that you're having them run a gauntlet instead of making the best use of their time. Some search committees will try to justify an overscheduled interview process by saying, "We just want people to know how busy we are around here and get a sense of whether they're up to the challenge." But that type of reasoning is really rather specious. Faculty members are busy at *all* institutions and, although you may think that your faculty members work harder than people do elsewhere, those people probably have the same misconception about you.

It's sometimes hard to remember during the interview process that the dynamics of your relationship with at least one of the finalists is likely to change quite soon. At the moment, you're in the power position: You have something they want (the job), and so they're trying to impress you. But once there is a decision about which candidate to hire, these positions are reversed: They have something you want (a willingness to sign the contract), and so you must try to impress them. That last task becomes all the more difficult if you ran your finalists ragged during the interview process and left them with the impression that your institution didn't care about them, didn't know how to run an efficient search, or both. One institution where I once interviewed for a deanship scheduled two full days of meetings that began with breakfast interviews at 7:00 AM and didn't conclude until late in the evening after a few selected campus activities with the search committee (a play one day and a departmental lecture the next) had concluded. The only thing I learned about that institution during the search process was that it was one place where I never wanted to work.

Building in sufficient free time to the interview process provides candidates with the leisure they need to prepare for their next meeting and to learn more about your institution and the community. They're sizing you up at the same time that you're sizing them up, and they need a bit of unscheduled time in order to do that. Give the candidates an opportunity to explore the institution on their own. Allow them to have at least one meal a day where someone doesn't ask a question every time they bring their fork close to their mouths. Provide some options because some candidates might prefer going to a football game rather than an art exhibit whereas others would choose cultural events over athletic activities. Don't take the candidates on a forced march through all of the institution's facilities and try to introduce them to as many people as possible. They won't remember even a tenth of those meetings if they end up working at your college or university a few months later. Those tours and introductions are usually better left to the orientation or onboarding process for new employees than during the search process when all the information the candidates are trying to process has little immediate relevance for them.

Achieving the proper balance between overscheduling and under-scheduling the interview process is easier if you adopt performance-based interviewing than the more traditional series of question-and-answer sessions with various individuals or groups. By focusing on what you *really* need to know about a finalist to determine whether he or she would be successful at the job, constructing a series of opportunities to find out whether the finalist has the skills and attributes you need, and then scheduling a single question-and-answer session open to all stakeholders near the end of the search, you're much more likely to set a schedule that provides you and the candidates what you most desire to know. (For more on overscheduling or underscheduling interviews, see Buller, 2012, pp. 172–174.)

## ○ information needed by the candidates

All candidates need to know the status of their application at various points throughout the process: whether their application is complete, whether it's still being actively considered, whether their references will be contacted, and so on. When a candidate is selected for an on-campus interview, however, his or her need for information increases significantly. In some cases, the on-campus visit may be the first real experience they have of the institution, and how they're treated can be a major factor in whether they'll accept a job offer if one is made. Among the answers that finalists for positions will need to know are the following:

- Whether they need to make travel arrangements themselves or whether those arrangements will be made for them (and by whom)
- What will be reimbursed and, if there are limits on reimbursements, what those limits are
- Who will be picking them up at the airport (or other location) and how they will recognize that person
- Where the person will be staying if the interview includes an overnight visit, along with contact information for that location
- If clothing other than standard business attire would be useful for any activity, suggestions about what to bring; for example, if attending a football game is an optional or expected activity, the candidate will not want to attend that event in a suit and tie or a business dress
- The schedule for the interview process
- Background information about the school and program or websites where that information is available
- Who will be present at each interview meeting to the extent that this can be known in advance (For the chair, search committee members,

and other administrators who will be involved in the process, a brief bio statement may be desirable.)

- Contact information if accommodations for a physical challenge are desired
- How to submit receipts for reimbursement
- Whom to contact throughout the travel and interview processes if a delay or other problem arises

○ information needed by the interviewers

Just as the finalists have need of certain information in order to make their best impression, so does everyone who will be interacting with the candidate need certain information in order to perform his or her tasks effectively. Remember that finalists don't just meet with the search committee. There are also likely to be encounters with other members of the faculty and staff, students, family members of institutional employees, realtors and other members of the community, advisory board members, and so on. Although it's impossible to predict everyone with whom a finalist will have an encounter, those who can be determined in advance should be given access to the following materials:

- The candidate's curriculum vitae
- The candidate's interview schedule
- Samples of the candidate's research or creative activity if applicable
- The job description of the position the candidate is being considered for
- Sections of any institutional handbooks or manuals related to faculty hiring
- A list of what can and should not be asked during a conversation with the candidate (See Chapter 5 for such a list.)
- Forms for providing impressions of the candidate to the search committee (See Appendix A.)

In addition, make sure that the rooms where meetings will take place are all reserved and that parking arrangements have been made for community members or others who don't have a campus parking pass. Also be sure that even those who are unlikely to be directly involved in the interview process understand that the interview is going on so that they can greet visitors appropriately and demonstrate their best professional behavior.

## ○ putting it all together

Many search committees believe that the entire search process can be improvised. The members of the committee don't plan any questions in advance and assume that they'll think of the right thing to ask when the moment comes. At the opposite extreme, other committees write out every question the candidates will be asked at each meeting, reading the questions precisely as they're written out so that they'll see how different candidates do when asked exactly the same things. Neither of these extremes is likely to yield the kind of insights you most need in order to increase the likelihood of success for the candidate you select. Two best practices are of key importance: First, performance-based interviewing tells you a lot more than do traditional questions and answers. Second, making interview processes comparable doesn't mean that you have to make them all identical. Some elements of each interview can be tailored to the specific needs and interests of different candidates. Just as you'd make reasonable accommodations in conducting an interview with a physically challenged applicant, so should interview processes include reasonable accommodations for *all* candidates, based on what will best tell the candidate what he or she needs to know about you and tell your institution what it needs to know about the candidate.

# 5

# conducting the interviews

In Chapter 4, we see that performance-based interviewing—a process whereby candidates *show* you what they can do; they don't just *tell* you—is far more effective than traditional question-and-answer interviewing in identifying the applicant who will best succeed in your environment. But even when they're aware of the merits of performance-based interviewing, most search committees still elect to conduct interviews in the familiar question-and-answer format. Why? One reason is that it simply *is* more familiar than alternative approaches. Search committees feel comfortable asking questions because they've done it many times before. Many search committee members got their jobs by way of a traditional interview, so that must be proof that the system works, right?

Another reason is that performance-based interviewing requires a lot more planning and preparation than merely asking questions. You have to come to consensus about all the skills, attributes, and attitudes a successful candidate is going to need and then discover creative ways to explore those. It can take ingenuity to develop ways of testing an applicant's collegiality, ability to take constructive criticism, dedication to a team approach, or any of the other factors that determine whether someone is the type of person a program needs. And many people decide that they don't have time for that during a busy academic term. So, even though they may have an intellectual awareness that merely looking for qualifications on a résumé and posing questions in an interview aren't particularly effective ways of selecting faculty members, they do so anyway.

This chapter is thus built on the premise that most colleges and universities will continue using traditional question-and-answer interviews in their search processes. At least, they'll incorporate a large number of interview questions into their processes even if they begin to implement performance-based interviewing. Our task, then, becomes the following: If most search committees are going to conduct interviews by asking questions despite knowing that this practice is highly flawed, how can we make it a little less flawed? In other words, if people are going to ask candidates questions, how can they ask better questions? Appendix B contains a number of questions that can help search committees gain greater insight into a candidate's strengths and weaknesses. But not even the longest list of sample interview questions can include every issue that you may want to know about, so let's explore ways in which you can craft questions to make the best use of the time your committee and the candidates are going to spend together.

Throughout this discussion of how to conduct interviews more effectively, we'll keep returning to five sample questions similar to those often asked during faculty interviews. We'll explore what's wrong with these questions and consider ways of making the questions better. The sample questions we'll use for this discussion are as follows:

1.  What's your greatest weakness?
2.  How would you describe your teaching style?
3.  What are your research plans for the next 5 to 10 years?
4.  Our program desperately needs someone to serve on the institution-wide strategic planning committee. If we hired you, would you be willing to do that?
5.  Would people describe you as collegial? A consensus-builder?

Throughout this discussion, I will suggest guidelines that can help turn these commonly asked but poor questions into more effective questions. In Chapter 4, we conducted a thought experiment about whether someone would learn more about a baker's skill by sampling his or her wares or by talking with the baker about the process of baking. Our five sample questions are all what we might call *process-of-baking questions.* Those are the types of questions people will know how to answer by asking themselves, "What would a good baker say in this situation?" In the case of our sample questions, a candidate is likely to tell you what he or she thinks you want to hear—that is, what a good colleague and faculty member would say—not necessarily what he or she really believes. As we've seen, candidates are on their best behavior during an interview. They're seeking to make a positive impression and to present themselves in the best possible light. They're unlikely to say anything that reveals a serious flaw or that would cause them to receive less consideration for the position. Indeed, if a candidate *does* suddenly start to provide overly candid and self-destructive answers, it may be a sign that he or she has already decided not to accept the job even if it's offered. You may want to begin gently exploring whether that is truly the case.

Interview questions tend to be more effective when, rather than being posed in a vague or general manner, they contain a specific, performance-based element. These performance-based elements include phrasings such as the following:

- Tell us about a time when . . .
- Describe a recent situation when . . .
- What were you thinking while . . . ?
- Guide me through your decision-making process when you . . .
- Give us an example of an instance when you . . .
- Identify three or four challenges when you had to . . .

By incorporating these elements, we can rephrase our five sample questions as follows:

1. Tell us about a time when a specific weakness caused you problems professionally and then discuss how you handled the situation.
2. Give us an example of an instance when you changed something in one of the courses you were teaching so that the students were engaged in more active learning.

3. Identify three or four challenges you had to overcome in your research so far and describe how you overcame them.

4. Guide me through your decision-making process when you decide which committees you'd like to serve on.

5. Describe a recent situation in which you had to build consensus. What caused the initial lack of agreement, and how did you respond?

Phrased in this way, the questions become requests for information and cause the candidate to talk about actual performance rather than generalities and "what a good professor would do." It's always possible, of course, that the candidate will simply lie, but now you'll have a specific incident that you can verify in any follow-up reference calls you make after the interview.

These performance-based questions provide better insight into the candidate's thought processes and behaviors than do most interview questions. And although there's no one way for a candidate to answer these questions correctly, there is one red flag for the search committee to look out for: a candidate who continually uses the same incident to answer many questions. That answer suggests that either the candidate hasn't had much experience (and thus doesn't have a large body of examples to draw on) or hasn't had a great deal of success in the areas you care most about. A lack of experience may be forgiven if the search is for an entry-level position, but a more seasoned candidate who can only think of one situation in which he or she responded effectively is perhaps not someone you'd want to hire for your program.

> When you're not conducting performance-based interviews, at least ask performance-based questions.

Another way of gaining insight into how a candidate might actually respond to a challenge or opportunity is to pose a hypothetical question. Hypothetical questions aren't uncommon in academic interviewing— and often the situations they describe aren't really hypothetical at all but descriptions of events that have actually happened with a few small details changed—but they often aren't used very effectively. Search committees frequently use hypothetical questions as *litmus tests*: If applicants answer "correctly," they're considered viable candidates; if they don't, they probably won't be offered the job. But regardless of how detailed the hypothetical scenario is, it can't provide the candidate with everything he or she needs to know in order to make the "right" choice. For example, the personalities of the people involved may have played a role in how the situation unfolded. Or certain elements of institutional culture of which the candidate is currently unaware may have influenced the outcome. Litmus test questions often force applicants to do little better than guess how they should respond, with serious consequences resting on the outcome of that guess.

The type of hypothetical questions that help the search committee gain real insights into the values and perspectives of the applicants are quite different from these litmus test questions. They're more concise and simply try to get the candidate to envision an actual situation rather than to think about an issue in more universal or philosophical terms. Here's how our five sample questions might be improved by basing them on hypothetical scenarios:

1.  Let's imagine that it's a few years from now, and a major crisis has arisen in the program because of what everyone recognizes is your greatest weakness. People are holding you responsible for the problem and expecting you to fix it. What problem may you have caused, and how do you go about undoing the damage?
2.  Assume for a moment that you're teaching a class you've taught many times before, but this particular group of students just can't seem to master the material. They seem as bright and capable as those in your previous classes, but their grades are low, and they appear to be disengaged from the material. How might you respond?
3.  Pretend for a moment that it's your fourth year on tenure track and, for whatever reason, your current research trajectory has hit a brick wall. Maybe the funding has dried up, or that particular research

area has suddenly fallen into disfavor, or something else has happened. You have only 2 years left before your tenure review. What do you do?

4. Imagine that you're having a particularly busy semester. You have a major research project to complete, and your portfolio for promotion and tenure is due by the end of the term. The department has just unanimously elected you to the institution-wide strategic planning committee, one of our most important but also most time-consuming committees. What do you do?

5. Suppose you had a senior colleague who was rude to you, even something of a bully. Other people are being treated the same way, and you notice that this person's behavior is having a chilling effect on department meetings. Even though this colleague holds a higher rank than you, what are some specific steps you might take to improve collegiality throughout the program?

These questions are far more difficult for a candidate to prepare for than standard interview questions and thus far more likely to prompt a candid, unrehearsed response. Because they immerse the candidate in a realistic (albeit fictional) situation, they call for more specific answers than do general questions and provide insight into the way a candidate deals with challenges.

> Rather than asking universal or philosophical questions, present hypothetical situations and ask for a response.

Everyone knows the questions that will probably come up during an interview. Someone will inevitably ask, "Why do you want this job?" and "What's your greatest weakness?" As a result, everyone knows how you're supposed to answer these questions: You try to make it sound as though this job is your dream job, the opportunity you've been preparing for all your life, and you try to make a weakness sound like a strength ("I just get too darn caught up in my work sometimes because

I want everything I do to be the best."). There are whole shelves of books that candidates can consult with titles such as *101 Job Interview Questions You'll Never Fear Again* (Reed, 2016) and *Best Answers to the 201 Most Frequently Asked Interview Questions* (DeLuca & DeLuca, 2010). These questions are perfectly fine to ask in the first few minutes of an interview when you're trying to get the candidate to relax and converse comfortably. But they shouldn't be the sum total of everything you discuss in the interview.

With a little bit of creativity, you can get at the same issues interviewers have in mind when they pose stock questions, but you'll be far less likely to receive a stock answer. Here's how we might revise our five sample questions by making them a little less hackneyed:

1. Let's imagine that it's 3 years from now, and this search committee is getting together again. We can all agree on one thing: "Hiring that candidate is the best decision we ever made, except for . . ." What are we likely to say after "except for"?

2. Suppose that one day this department names a faculty teaching award after you because your distinctive—even unique—teaching style revolutionized the way we teach our discipline. What will your big innovation have been?

3. Pretend that we're not at the beginning of your career here but at the end. It's your retirement party, and I've been charged with giving a speech about the contributions you've made to our discipline in research. What do you hope I'll say?

4. If our institution-wide strategic planning committee asked you for advice on how to develop and implement the school's next strategic plan, what three recommendations would you make?

5. Imagine that we're not the search committee but the departmental tenure and promotion committee. It's 6 years from now, and we're reviewing your application. One of our members points out that you did three things in your first 6 years here that really boosted morale and improved collegiality in the program. What three things will that person probably mention?

Creativity is involved in these questions, not only because they pose commonly asked questions in innovative ways but also because they prompt the candidates to be creative themselves. Note, too, that they incorporate one simple technique to move candidates away from their rehearsed answers: They don't ask for a single example. Everyone who prepares for an interview has one example in mind for most of the stock questions that are posed. Ask for three to five examples.

> Whenever possible, steer clear of trite or stock interview questions.

It's not at all uncommon during interviews to hear people asking questions that virtually beg candidates to answer in a particular way. "Are you a team player? Are you willing to teach the introductory courses that we so desperately need? Would you be willing to include an exceptionally well-prepared undergraduate on your research team?" Unless a candidate is absolutely obtuse, he or she will understand immediately that the only acceptable answer to these questions is *yes*. Certainly, obtuse candidates do exist but there's no need to ask special questions to identify them; they become obvious by their answers to even more effectively phrased questions.

As a general practice, open-ended questions are always better choices for interviews than yes-or-no questions, leading questions, or questions with only a very small number of possible answers. With this guideline in mind, we might reconstruct our five sample questions as follows:

1.  What weakness do you believe most often undermines the success of faculty members, and how do you take steps to avoid developing that weakness yourself?
2.  What kind of teaching style is most effective with today's students, and how have you used that style in your own courses?
3.  As you reflect on how your academic specialty is likely to develop over the next 5 to 10 years, what do you envision the major themes

or areas of interest are likely to be? How do you see your own work fitting into those themes or areas of research?

4. Even though we often focus on teaching and research as the most important responsibilities a faculty member has, service to the institution and the profession is also a critical component in faculty success. In your view, what would constitute an appropriate level of service for a tenure-track faculty member? Be specific by providing a few examples of committees and other service contributions you think a tenure-track faculty member should be expected to make.

5. What attributes or interpersonal skills do you believe faculty members need to succeed in today's challenging environment for higher education? If you can, please provide us with several examples of how you've demonstrated those attributes or skills in your own work.

In this way, the questions you ask don't feed candidates the right or expected answer but try to solicit the candidates' views, while still asking for specific examples to corroborate that they actually practice what they preach.

> Avoid any question that appears to have clear right or wrong answers.

There is, however, one time for which a simple yes-or-no question with a clearly correct answer is appropriate: when you're asking about something that's an absolute requirement for the job. For example, an interviewer (who for this type of question will usually be either the chair or the dean) might phrase a question in this way: "As you'll have noticed in the ad, the person we hire for this position is going to be expected to teach at least two sections of English composition every single semester. We've had some difficulty in the past because people were hired to teach composition, and then assumed they could replace this assignment with literature courses after several years. So, I need you to acknowledge that you understand that the person hired into this position will be predominantly or even exclusively assigned composition courses to teach and that this assignment will not change. Do you agree to that?" In this case, the question isn't really an interview question through which one is trying to gain insight into the candidate's qualifications and personal style. Instead, it's a contract commitment question in which a supervisor is trying to solicit a commitment that the potential employee would agree to abide by the required terms of the job.

## ○ the purpose of campus interviews

As our discussion of interview questions suggests, many search committees waste a great opportunity in the way they conduct campus interviews. Rather than finding more about what the candidate can contribute to their programs, they resort to unimaginative questions for which every applicant is prepared and has ready (if not always honest) answers. They fail to ask themselves these fundamental questions: "Why, in this day of widespread electronic communications, do we even have face-to-face interviews? Why not simply save the expense of bringing the candidate in by asking all the questions stakeholders have by videoconference and draw conclusions in that way?"

The response is that there are still many aspects of who a candidate is and how he or she interacts with others that are still best determined by a campus interview. Moreover, unless the faculty member will be conducting research remotely and teaching all of his or her classes online, the work that a faculty member does will largely be performed on campus and involve personal interactions with many different types of stakeholders. For this reason, the unique opportunities that are possible in a face-to-face interview should provide the basis for which questions to ask.

> As a general rule, apply the following touchstone to determine what you need to do during an on-campus interview with a candidate: What do I need to know about this person that I can learn best through a face-to-face interview?

By applying this principle, you may well find yourself wanting to replace many of the typical question-and-answer sessions found in most campus interviews with the performance-based approach I share in Chapter 4. In addition, you may want to include many more stakeholder groups in the interview process than commonly occurs. For example, if much of your community support is derived from relatively elderly patrons, you don't want to wait until after a candidate is hired to discover that he or she is abrupt or insensitive in conversations with them. If a faculty member will have to teach a number of general education courses, you don't want to derive a false impression of his or her teaching style by observing a sample class that contains only graduate students.

Moreover, as you think about the opportunities accorded by an on-campus interview, you may well conclude that the *content* of the candidate's answers matters far less than his or her *style*. You can learn what a candidate knows in a wide variety of ways: telephone interviews, video conferences, reference calls, written responses to specific questions, e-mail exchanges, and so on. So, by the time a candidate arrives on campus, there should be no question about the person's qualifications. You should already know that, regardless of which finalist is selected, that person will be *capable* of doing the job. What you can determine only in person is the candidate's overall fit with the program— not in the sense of a code word for "just like us" that I mention in Chapter 1 but in the sense of the best choice for taking the program where it needs to go. Smart search committees are on the alert for how the candidate interacts with people, what seems to cause the candidate an unreasonable amount of annoyance, with whom the candidate seems to develop an instant rapport, and why he or she responds favorably to certain aspects of the program and less favorably to others.

It's also a waste of time during the on-campus interview to revisit issues that have already been sufficiently covered elsewhere in the process. Follow-up questions about matters that were unclear or that seem contradicted by some of the candidate's other answers are fair game. But don't abuse the candidate's patience—or that of the search committee—by continuing to reassess material that was satisfactorily covered in previous parts of the process.

> During on-campus interviews, don't repeat questions that were already covered in phone interviews or elsewhere. If you need to return to a subject, look for ways of probing into it more deeply.

## ○ "Illegal" Interview Questions

People involved with searches in higher education often speak of "illegal" interview questions and warn that, if anyone asks one of these questions during an interview, the process will immediately be compromised, the search aborted, and the position possibly lost. That's a bit of an overreaction. We need to begin by recognizing that *there are no such things as illegal interview questions and no question can automatically cause a search to become invalid.* What does exist is a category we might call *inadvisable interview questions* because asking them can cause a search's legitimacy to be challenged and, depending on other factors, put the outcome in jeopardy.

Here's what makes an interview question inadvisable. If an interviewer appears to be trying to determine whether a candidate falls into a protected class (on the concept of protected classes, see Chapter 1), there may be a presumption by applicants not hired for the position that inappropriate reasons were used in making the hiring decision. For example, let's engage in a thought experiment.

Imagine that you live in an alternate universe in which there has been a history of discrimination against people born in the spring. Out of basic fairness and because institutions had long been depriving themselves of the talents and contributions of people with vernal birthdays, people born in the spring are now a protected class. Application forms no longer have spaces for candidates to list their birthdays, and employers are cautioned against bringing up this issue during interviews.

You're happy about this situation because your birthday is in April, and you've had trouble getting a job. One day you're being interviewed for what appears to be the perfect job for you at Seasonal State

University, and everything is going well—except for one uncomfortable moment while having lunch with several of the deans. Near the end of the meal, one of the deans says, "We have a little custom here at Seasonal State. The person whose birthday is the closest gets to choose what we all have for dessert. Mine is September 9th, Carla's is December 3rd, and Dave's is August 24th. So, when's yours?"

The question makes you a little uncomfortable, and you demur a bit, saying that you're really not interested in dessert anyway. The dean who seems to be in charge keeps pressing you, however, and you try to get out of the situation by making what seems to you to be a light and friendly remark about inappropriate questions during an interview. But the dean won't let up. "Oh, we're all just having lunch together, and it's all in good fun. When did you say your birthday was?"

It's become awkward to keep refusing to answer, so you mention your birthday and—surprise!—you get to choose dessert for everyone at the table. The uncomfortable moment passes. But then, several weeks later, you receive a letter thanking you for applying to Seasonal State University but informing you that another candidate has been hired. Because your interview went so well and everyone on the search committee seemed so enthusiastic about your candidacy, you can't quite get the thought out of your mind: Did that incident at lunch cost me this job? You don't really believe so, but you also can't be 100% sure. Jobs are scarce in your field, and you badly need employment, so what do you do?

You may be experiencing a sense of uncertainty after conducting this thought experiment. Should you raise the issue with the university or perhaps even file a complaint? If you do, what outcome can you reasonably expect? The job has already been given to someone else, and you can't prove that you would've been hired if your birthday weren't in the spring. If you don't, aren't you tacitly lending support to a culture of discrimination and making it harder for the next person who happens to be in your same situation?

This thought experiment reveals why it's inadvisable to ask any questions that touch on whether an applicant may be a member of a protected class. And notice one other element of the thought experiment:

The question didn't arise during what many people would consider to be a formal part of the interview. It happened during what seemed to be a moment of casual conversation. So, it isn't just members of the search committee who need to be informed about what areas of conversation are best avoided during the interview. Anyone who may meet the candidate socially, such as friends or family members of those who work at the institution if they may encounter the candidate during a social event, should also be cautioned about inappropriate questions.

As I discuss in Chapter 1, which groups count as protected classes during a search will depend on where your school is located and its mission. For example, a private institution with a strong religious mission is certainly free to ask about a candidate's faith if it's an important aspect of the job, but that type of question would be completely inappropriate at a state institution. For this reason, Table 5.1 is only a guideline for what may constitute an inappropriate question at most colleges and universities in the United States. Because your own situation may well be different, be sure to check with human resources or the provost's office in order to determine the precise composition of protected classes at your school.

In addition, even a number of seemingly innocuous questions have at times been viewed as inadvisable because of how people may interpret them. For instance, most people would find questions such as "Do you have your own car?" or "Do you rent where you live now or have your own home?" to be innocent enough. But to members of a minority group who have struggled to free themselves of the stereotype that they are all poor and live in ghettos, such questions may sound completely different. A general rule of thumb is that questions should either be directly relevant to the job in question or, in social situations, generic, open-ended questions such as the following:

- What sorts of things do you like to do when you're not working?
- How was your trip to our area? Did you have any delays or problems while you were traveling?

**Table 5.1 Protected Classes and Inappropriate Interview Questions**

| Protected Class | Examples of Inappropriate Questions | Examples of Permissible Questions |
|---|---|---|
| Age | <ul><li>What year were you born?</li><li>What year did you graduate high school?</li><li>Does college seem to have changed a lot since you attended?</li></ul><ul><li>Those are very impressive credentials for someone your age! When did you start teaching?</li><li>Why would you want to move so far away from home when you'll be retiring in a few years?</li></ul><ul><li>When do you plan to retire?</li><li>What lovely gray hair. Is that natural?</li></ul> | None. In certain types of employment, it may be necessary to determine whether the candidate is old enough to work legally in that profession, but that issue doesn't apply to faculty positions. |
| Gender | <ul><li>How shall I refer to you: as he or as she?</li><li>Have you ever been sexually harassed?</li><li>As a [man or woman], how do you feel about . . .?</li></ul> | None. |
| Sexual orientation | <ul><li>What can you tell me about any significant other in your life?</li><li>Your style of dress seems rather unusual for a [woman or man]. Why do you dress that way?</li><li>Why are you wearing that earring?</li></ul> | None. |

*(Continued)*

**Table 5.1** (*Continued*)

| Protected Class | Examples of Inappropriate Questions | Examples of Permissible Questions |
|---|---|---|
| **Marital status** | • What is your spouse's name?<br>• What does your spouse do?<br>• Will your spouse be coming with you if you take this job?<br>• You say you live with a roommate. Can you clarify that relationship?<br>• Is that an engagement or wedding ring I see?<br>• What is your maiden name?<br>• How shall I address you: Miss or Mrs.? | None. |
| **Family status** | • Are you planning to have (additional) children?<br>• What are your childcare arrangements? Who watches your children while you're at work?<br>• How many times have you been married?<br>• Are you currently in a committed relationship?<br>• How does your spouse feel about your job? | • If certain work hours are required for the job and you pose the question to all finalists, you may ask questions such as "The person holding this position will need to teach a 9:00 AM and a 3:00 PM class on Monday, Wednesday, and Friday, as well as a Tuesday-Thursday class at 2:30 PM. Would you be able to do that?"<br>• If travel is a required aspect of the job, you may ask about the candidate's ability and willingness to travel. |

**Table 5.1** (*Continued*)

| Protected Class | Examples of Inappropriate Questions | Examples of Permissible Questions |
|---|---|---|
| **Race** | • What is your ancestry?<br>• Are both of your parents [members of a specific race]?<br>• Any question about a candidate's height, complexion, skin color, or eye color. | None. |
| **National origin** | • What is your ancestry?<br>• In what country were you born?<br>• Are both of your parents [members of a specific nationality]?<br>• How long has your family been in this country?<br>• That's an interesting name. What does it mean? (Or what are its origins?)<br>• How did you learn to speak [name of language]?<br>• Where did you get that accent?<br>• What's your native language? | • Are you legally authorized to work in this country?<br>• If proficiency in a specific language is a requirement for the job, you may inquire into the person's level of fluency in that language or provide a skills test. |

(*Continued*)

**Table 5.1** (*Continued*)

| Protected Class | Examples of Inappropriate Questions | Examples of Permissible Questions |
|---|---|---|
| **Religion** | • Which holidays will you be celebrating?<br>• Do you attend church [or any other type of religious service] regularly?<br>• In the space on the application form marked "Religion," what would you like me to fill in for you?<br>• Did you go to public or religious schools?<br>• We have quite a number of interesting religious organizations here. Would you like to hear about any of them?<br>• What a lovely [piece of religious jewelry]! Why do you wear it? | If weekend work is required for the job and you pose the question to all finalists, you may ask questions such as "Can you work on weekends?" |
| **Physical challenges** | • Do you have any physical disabilities?<br>• Do you always need to use your walker, wheelchair, other accommodation?<br>• Are you completely or only partially blind or deaf? | If you pose the question to all finalists, you may ask questions such as "Will you be able to perform the essential functions of this position, either with or without reasonable accommodations?" |

**Table 5.1** (*Continued*)

| Protected Class | Examples of Inappropriate Questions | Examples of Permissible Questions |
|---|---|---|
| **Medical history** | • Do you have any preexisting medical conditions?<br>• What medications do you use?<br>• How much do you weigh?<br>• Do you use drugs or alcohol?<br>• Do you smoke?<br>• How did you get that scar?<br>• Have you ever filed for workers' compensation?<br>• How much sick leave have you used in previous jobs?<br>• Do you need to visit doctors frequently?<br>• How is your family's health?<br>• Do you exercise regularly? | • If you pose the question to all finalists, you may ask questions such as "Will you be able to perform the essential functions of this position, either with or without reasonable accommodations?"<br>• If the campus is dry or smoke free, you may mention these policies to all finalists. |
| **Veteran status** | • Was your discharge from the military honorable or dishonorable?<br>• Do you have any lingering effects from your service?<br>• How do you alleviate the anxieties and pressures that stem from your military service? | • If it is relevant to the job, you may ask about special training the candidate received or skills that he or she developed while in the military.<br>• If the candidate has self-disclosed that he or she served in the military, you may ask in which branch the candidate served. (That question is<br>(*Continued*) |

**Table 5.1** (*Continued*)

| Protected Class | Examples of Inappropriate Questions | Examples of Permissible Questions |
|---|---|---|
| | • How often will your reserve duties take you away from the job? | more likely to arise in social situations than in formal interviews, however, because it is probably unrelated to job responsibilities.) |
| Criminal history | • Have you ever been arrested?<br>• Have you ever been pulled over for drunk driving?<br>• Have you ever spent a night in jail? | • Have you ever been convicted of a crime?<br>• If it is the case at your institution, you may say, "Our institution runs background checks on anyone we're seriously considering for a job. If we believe we're about to make you an offer, we'll check with you to determine whether that's okay with you." |
| Affiliations | • What clubs do you belong to?<br>• Which political parties have you joined? | If certain professional organizations are relevant to the job, you may ask about a candidate's membership status and activity in those organizations. |

- What first got you interested in a career in higher education?
- What's one thing about you that I might not expect?
- Do you have any favorite restaurants near where you live now?

Good questions to ask in social situations are ones that enable candidates to be as open or reserved as they like and that won't lead to an awkward silence by seeming to press the candidates for information they'd prefer not to share. Notice that you don't want to ask candidates what hobbies they have or which organizations they belong to, because certain hobbies and organizations have implicit connection with gender, ethnicity, and other personal characteristics. It's better to keep the question broader and general by asking about a person's interests or favorite activities outside of work, because then the candidate can decide in which direction to take the question.

> If an issue isn't related to the job, don't ask it during formal interview sessions. In more social settings, keep the topics of conversation general and respect the candidates' right to share as much or as little as they wish.

If you discover that an inappropriate question has been asked, there are several things you'll need to do. First, find out who posed the question and have a conversation with that person about why the question was inappropriate; then, inform the person not to ask such a question again. In truly egregious situations, you might consider removing that person from any further participation in the search process. Second, inform your supervisor and the office of human resources what has occurred and work out with them a plan for proceeding. Third, unless instructed not to do so by either your supervisor or the office of human resources, have a candid conversation with the applicant about the situation. Make it clear that you, along with everyone else involved in the search process, recognizes that the question was inappropriate and that it will have absolutely no bearing on the decision about whom to hire. If your supervisor or the human resources representative instructs you not to discuss the issue with the applicant, inquire into the reasons for this recommendation. It may well be that the issue has already been fully addressed with the candidate, and so there's no need to dredge up a matter that's already been resolved. But if you sense that the person merely wants to cover up an inappropriate action or conceal from the candidate something that can affect the legitimacy of the search, it may be best to consider checking with your campus's legal counsel for their advice on how you should proceed.

## o   the conclusion of the interview

Although interviews can take almost any shape that best serves the interests of the institution or program, it's almost always desirable to conclude the process with a one-on-one exit interview with the search chair, department chair, or dean. This exit interview enables the candidate to express any concerns he or she may have about how the interview was conducted or how he or she was treated. It enables the person conducting the meeting to ask the finalist if he or she has any last questions or any concerns that might prevent him or her from taking the position if it is offered. If the topic hasn't yet arisen, the person in charge of the meeting can also ask whether the candidate is actively involved in any other searches or has any other factors affecting the timetable in which he or she can make a decision. The exit interview should be an attempt to end the interview process on a cordial, friendly note. Even if it's already clear to everyone concerned that this finalist will not be offered the job, there is no benefit to be derived from leaving this person with a poor impression. He or she may convey that impression to others, have children or grandchildren who won't attend the institution because of how the candidate was treated, or react in other ways that cast the program in a poor light. Even if the candidate is the last person you'd ever want to be your colleague, you've at least had the advantage of getting to know another person and gain insights into his or her perspectives. That experience is always valuable even if it doesn't cause you to hire the candidate.

## ○  putting it all together

Even though traditional interviews are not the most effective ways of selecting the best candidate for a position, most colleges and universities will continue to use them instead of engaging in practices such as performance-based interviewing. For this reason, it's important that the questions you ask be as effective as possible. By following the general guidelines that appear throughout this chapter and avoiding questions that may lead you into inappropriate areas, you increase your likelihood of posing questions that provide insight into which candidates are or are not good fits for the position, program, and institution.

No set of guidelines can ensure that search committees will recommend the best possible candidate in every search. However, the practices I've outlined in this book have been proven in many searches at colleges and universities both large and small, public and private, well established and newly emerging. With this sort guide in the hands of each member of the faculty search committee, you'll increase the likelihood that the application reviews and interviews you conduct are fair, proceed in a timely manner, and yield results that best serve the interest of your program. No decision you make will affect your department or college more than whom you hire, so follow these best practices to make the wisest possible choices.

# appendix a: candidate evaluation form

A standardized rating form for candidates makes it easier to compare reactions that different observers have to the same applicant. Although you'll want to modify the form to suit the precise needs of your institution and program, the following example provides a good starting point to indicate how a candidate evaluation form might be constructed. The form enables people to submit a single evaluation based on several separate interactions with the candidate. Best practices indicate, however, that evaluators should complete and submit a separate form after each interaction with the candidate. In that way, if people's responses for one type of interaction (for example, a meal with the candidate) are significantly different from those associated with other types of interaction (such as phone interviews and formal presentations), the search committee will have better insight into possible reasons why these outliers occurred. Similarly, although best practices suggest that candid responses are more likely when forms are submitted anonymously, some demographic information is collected so that it can be determined whether one stakeholder group had a different response to the candidate than did other stakeholder groups.

## Candidate Evaluation Form

**Search:** _____

After completing this form, please return it to _____ no later than

_____.

---

Your role on the search committee:

☐  search committee member

☐  not a search committee member

---

Your connection to the institution:

☐  faculty member

☐  staff member

☐  student

☐  administrator

☐  community member

☐  other (please specify): _____

---

If you are a faculty member, do you work in the department or program that will employ this faculty member?

☐  yes

☐  no

☐  not applicable

This evaluation is based on the following (check all that apply):

☐  Review of the candidate's application materials

☐  Phone or video interview with the candidate (circle which type)

☐  The candidate's letters of recommendation

☐  Phone or video conversations with the candidate's references (circle which type)

☐  A meal with the candidate

- ☐  A one-on-one meeting with the candidate
- ☐  A small meeting or Q+A session (25 or fewer people) with the candidate
- ☐  A large meeting or Q+A session (more than 25 people) with the candidate
- ☐  A sample class taught by the candidate
- ☐  A research presentation made by the candidate
- ☐  A casual or passing encounter with the candidate
- ☐  Other (please specify): _____

---

Please rate the candidate in any of the following areas you wish. Use the right-most column if you were unable to judge (**NJ**) the candidate's performance in that area or have no opinion (**NO**) about the candidate's performance in that area. Any item left blank will also be considered as **NJ/NO**.

|  | Excellent | Good | Fair | Unsatisfactory | NJ/NO |
|---|---|---|---|---|---|
| Potential for excellence in teaching |  |  |  |  |  |
| Potential for excellence in research |  |  |  |  |  |
| Potential for excellence in service |  |  |  |  |  |
| Relevant qualifications for this position |  |  |  |  |  |
| Relevant experience for this position |  |  |  |  |  |
| Interpersonal skills |  |  |  |  |  |
| Likely fit with institutional mission and goals |  |  |  |  |  |
| Likely fit with programmatic mission and goals |  |  |  |  |  |

| | Excellent | Good | Fair | Unsatisfactory | NJ/NO |
|---|---|---|---|---|---|
| Likelihood of bringing diversity to the program | | | | | |
| Likelihood of bringing new vision to the program | | | | | |
| Likelihood of introducing curricular innovation | | | | | |
| Likelihood of introducing pedagogical innovation | | | | | |
| Likelihood of producing appropriate amounts of peer-reviewed research | | | | | |
| Likelihood of winning appropriate amounts of external grant support | | | | | |
| Likelihood of serving on needed committees | | | | | |
| Likelihood of being a good institutional citizen | | | | | |
| Other (please specify): | | | | | |

Include any comments you wish to make about the preceding rankings:

_____

_____

_____

The candidate's greatest strengths appear to be: _____

_____

The candidate's greatest weaknesses appear to be: _____

_____

Other comments you wish to make: _____

_____

_____

Based on your overall impressions of the candidate and your previous responses, which of the following statements is closest to your recommendation at this point in the search? (Choose only one.)

☐  I strongly recommend that this applicant remain a viable candidate.

☐  I recommend that this applicant remain a viable candidate.

☐  I recommend with reservations that this applicant remain a viable candidate. (State reservations.) _____

_____

☐  I do not recommend that this applicant remain a viable candidate.

*The search committee thanks you for your participation in this important process. Your perspective and recommendations will be given serious and thorough consideration.*

# appendix b: suggested interview questions

Competition for highly qualified faculty members is more intense than ever. With the demand for postsecondary education increasing all over the world, even universities that previously never saw themselves as vying with universities thousands of miles away now find that highly desirable candidates are applying at institutions internationally. As a result, it has become more important than ever to find ways of determining which applicants are the best fit for a particular position at a particular university in a particular region.

One of the most effective strategies academic leaders can adopt to discover which applicants are the right fit for their needs is to ask questions that go far beyond those typically asked during an academic search. All too often, administrators and search committees interview candidates about issues that do not extend much deeper than the information on the curriculum vitae itself. That practice is perfectly natural: We're interested, after all, in the applicant's research, record of teaching, and experience in university service. But years of teaching, number of refereed articles, and size of grants received tell only part of the story. Here are a few questions that academic leaders might well consider asking in order to identify those candidates who best suit the needs of the university, program, and university system as a whole.

## Questions About Teaching

- Who were your three most memorable students? What made them memorable?
- What have you done to make learning in your courses active rather than passive? Please give an example.
- What are students likely to gain from a course you've taught that they probably wouldn't gain from someone else teaching the same course?
- If you were to teach our [name of course], which textbook would you use? Why would you adopt that particular textbook?

## Questions About Research

- What was the most important thing you ever learned from a research project that failed?
- If you had to rely on only three sources to keep up with developments in your field, what would they be?
- In what areas do you see your own line of research growing in the future? Why are those areas worth pursuing?
- What is the perfect research environment? Please describe.

## Questions About Service

- Which committee appointments have you had so far that gave you the greatest sense of satisfaction? Which appointments did you enjoy least?
- How do you set priorities for your time given there are so many demands on you for teaching, research, and service?
- If you were to look back on a meeting and think, "Now, *that* was a great meeting," what is likely to have brought you to that conclusion?
- If your supervisor assigned you a service task that you personally thought was not the best use of your time, what would you do?

## Questions About Collegiality

- Reflect on the colleague or fellow student whom you regarded as the most irritating, difficult, or frustrating. What did this person do that bothered you?

- If you were to come here, what are you likely to miss most about where you are now?
- Imagine that, a year from now, we look back on hiring you and say, "That was the best hire we ever made." What is likely to have brought us to that conclusion?
- How would you describe your colleagues from your last position?

### Questions About Institutional Mission
- What is the greatest challenge facing college professors today?
- What is it about this particular position that attracts you the most?
- What has been your least successful work experience? Why did that situation come to mind?
- What have I forgotten to ask you?

### Other Discussion Areas for the Candidate
- Describe a situation in which you were able to use persuasion to convince someone to see things your way.
- Give me a specific example of a time when you were able to resolve a conflict.
- Tell me about a time you were able to deal successfully with another person even though that person didn't like you (or vice versa).
- Describe a situation in which you had to deal with an upset colleague.

### Questions and Discussion Areas for the Candidate's References
- What is X like when frustrated, angry, or annoyed?
- Describe a situation in which X's ideas were opposed or rejected by others.
- Describe what X was like when you saw his or her behavior at its worst.
- How does X respond when dealing with demanding students? Parents? Supervisors? Colleagues?

Some of these questions and discussion areas are designed to discover whether the candidate's expectations match the current needs of the university. For example, if the candidate describes an ideal research environment that could not be offered by the institution, even in a partial manner, then it is likely that this candidate may soon become dissatisfied with the resources and opportunities that you have available. If the applicant describes aspects of his or her least successful work experience that are likely to have parallels in the position you're offering, either the program or the candidate (and probably both) will soon find the situation frustrating. If the type of colleagues and service opportunities that have frustrated the candidate in the past are similar to those that he or she will encounter in the current job, then it is likely that the person will not be the best fit for the job.

In general, therefore, search committees use interview questions to accomplish the following:

- Uncover things that they'd never learn from the résumé itself
- Ask questions for which the applicant is unlikely to have a rehearsed response
- Explore the issues that relate most closely to whether a faculty member succeeds or fails at the tasks central to the duties assigned

# references and resources

## Works Cited

Buller, J. L. (2012). *The essential department chair: A comprehensive desk reference.* San Francisco, CA: Jossey-Bass.

Buller, J. L. (2015). *The essential academic dean or provost: A comprehensive desk reference.* San Francisco, CA: Jossey-Bass.

Columbia University Office of the Provost. (n.d.). *Guide to best practices in faculty search and hiring.* Retrieved from http://facultydiversity.columbia.edu/files/viceprovost/content/guide_to_best_practices_in_faculty_search_and_hiring.pdf

Conway, J. M., Jako, R. A., & Goodman, D. F. (1995). A meta-analysis of interrater and internal consistency reliability of selection interviews. *Journal of Applied Psychology, 80*(5), 565–579.

DeLuca, M. J., & DeLuca, N. F. (2010). *Best answers to the 201 most frequently asked interview questions.* New York, NY: McGraw-Hill.

The George Washington University. (n.d.). GW faculty diversity advocates responsibilities and guidelines. Retrieved from https://smhs.gwu.edu/diversity/sites/diversity/files/Faculty%20Diversity%20Advocate_Responsibilities%20and%20Guidelines.pdf

Gross, N. (2013). *Why are professors liberal and why do conservatives care?* Cambridge, MA: Harvard University Press.

Harvard University. (2016). Best practices for conducting faculty searches. Retrieved from http://faculty.harvard.edu/files/fdd/files/best_practices_for_conducting_faculty_searches_v1.2.pdf /files/downloads/Sample%20Candidate%20Evaluation%20Sheet.pdf

Hochel, S., & Wilson, C. E. (2007). *Hiring right: Conducting successful searches in higher education.* San Francisco, CA: Jossey-Bass.

Hosoda, M., Stone-Romero, E. F., & Coats, G. (2003). The effects of physical attractiveness on job-related outcomes: A meta-analysis of experimental studies. *Personnel Psychology, 56*(2), 431–462.

Hurtado, S., Eagan, K., Pryor, J. H., Whang, H., & Tran, S. (2012). *Undergraduate teaching faculty: The 2010–2011 HERI faculty survey.* Los Angeles, CA: University of California, Los Angeles, Higher Education Research Institute, Graduate School of Education & Information Studies.

Jaschik, S. (2012). Moving further to the left. *Inside Higher Ed.* Retrieved from https://www.insidehighered.com/news/2012/10/24/survey-finds-professors-already-liberal-have-moved-further-left

Jennings, M. K., & Stoker, L. (2008). Another and longer look at the impact of higher education on political involvement and attitudes. *Conference Papers—Midwestern Political Science Association* (pp. 1–52). Chicago, IL: Midwest Political Science Association.

June, A. W. (2015). The invisible labor of minority professors. *The Chronicle of Higher Education, 52*(11), A32–A35.

Kimball, R. (2008). *Tenured radicals: How politics has corrupted our higher education.* Chicago, IL: Ivan R. Dee.

Kurtz, H. (2005). College faculties a most liberal lot, study finds. *The Washington Post.* Retrieved from http://www.washingtonpost.com/wp-dyn/articles/A8427-2005Mar28.html

Maloney, E. C., & On the Fence Films. (2004). *Indoctrinate U.* New York, NY: On the Fence Films.

Mariani, M. D., & Hewitt, G. J. (2008). Indoctrination U.? Faculty ideology and changes in student political orientation. *PS: Political Science & Politics, 41*(4), 773–783.

McDaniel, M. A., Whetzel, D. L., Schmidt, F. L., & Maurer, S. D. (1994). The validity of employment interviews: A comprehensive review and meta-analysis. *Journal of Applied Psychology, 79*(4), 599–616.

National Center for Education Statistics. (n.d.). *Fast facts.* Retrieved from https://nces.ed.gov/fastfacts/display.asp?id=61

Office for Faculty Equity & Welfare. (n.d.). *Creating the search plan.* University of California at Berkeley. Retrieved from http://ofew.berkeley.edu/recruitment/non-senate-searches/creating-search-plan

Office of Diversity, Equity, and Access. (2015). *Guidelines and procedures for academic appointments.* University of Illinois. Retrieved from www.diversity.illinois.edu/NewSearchManual/search_guidelines_and_procedures.pdf

Reed, J. (2016). *101 job interview questions you'll never fear again.* East Rutherford, NJ: Penguin.

San Jose State University. (2015). *Academic finalist interview evaluation form.* Retrieved from http://www.sjsu.edu/facultyaffairs/docs/AcademicFinalistInterview-Evaluation2015.doc

Schmidt, F. L., & Hunter, J. E. (1998). The validity and utility of selection methods in personnel psychology: Practical and theoretical implications of 85 years of research findings. *Psychological Bulletin, 124*(2), 262–274.

Shapiro, B. (2004). *Brainwashed: How universities indoctrinate America's youth.* Nashville, TN: WND Books.

State of Maryland Commission on Civil Rights. (n.d.). Employment discrimination. Retrieved from mccr.maryland.gov/employmentdiscrimination.html

Sullivan, J. (2012). What's wrong with interviews? The top 50 most common interview problems. *ERE Recruiting Intelligence.* Retrieved from www.eremedia.com/ere/whats-wrong-with-interviews-the-top-50-most-common-interview-problems/

University of California at Berkeley. (n.d.). *Sample candidate evaluation form.* Retrieved from http://ofew.berkeley.edu/sites/default/files/non-senate_sample_candidate_evaluation_form.pdf

University of Chicago Human Resources. (n.d.). Forms, policies, & guides. Retrieved from humanresources.uchicago.edu/fpg/guides/managerstoolkit/diversity/professional.shtml

University of Florida. (n.d.). *Faculty candidate assessment form.* Retrieved from www.uflib.ufl.edu/committees/recruitment/Candidate_Assessment.doc

University of Michigan ADVANCE Program. (2015–2016). *Academic affairs hiring manual* (p. 22). Retrieved from advance.umich.edu/resources/toolkit.pdf

University of Pennsylvania. (n.d.). *Candidate evaluation sheet.* Retrieved from www.upenn.edu/provost/images/uploads/Candidate.Eval_.pdf

University of Virginia, Office of University Advancement. (n.d.). Manager's toolkit: Candidate evaluation. Retrieved from http://im.dev.virginia.edu/wp/managertoolkit/candidate-evaluation/

U.S. Census Bureau. (n.d.). QuickFacts: United States. Retrieved from http://quickfacts.census.gov/qfd/states/00000.html

*U.S. News & World Report.* (2016). Campus ethnic diversity: National universities. Retrieved from http://colleges.usnews.rankingsandreviews.com/best-colleges/rankings/national-universities/campus-ethnic-diversity

## Materials for Further Study

Buller, J. L. (2010). *The essential college professor: A practical guide to an academic career.* San Francisco, CA: Jossey-Bass.

Buller, J. L. (2011a). The need for linking innovation, creativity, and entrepreneurship. *Academic Leader, 27*(5), 4–5.

Buller, J. L. (2011b). Strategic hiring: Aligning personnel decisions with long-term institutional objectives. *Academic Leader, 27*(8), 3, 8.

Buller, J. L. (2014). What every search committee will tell you. *Academic Leader, 30*(3), 4–5.

Buller, J. L., & Cipriano, R. E. (2015). *A toolkit for college professors*. Lanham, MD: Rowman & Littlefield.

Chun, E., & Evans, A. (2015). Strategies for enhancing diversity in the academic department. *The Department Chair, 26*(2), 20–21.

Falcone, P. (2009). *96 great interview questions to ask before you hire*. (2nd ed.) New York, NY: AMACOM.

Hodgson, S. (2015). *Brilliant answers to tough interview questions*. (5th ed.) New York, NY: Pearson.

Hoevemeyer, V. A. (2006). *High-impact interview questions: 701 behavior-based questions to find the right person for every job*. New York, NY: AMACOM.

# Index

Faculty searches: affirmative action and equal opportunity role in, 6–10, 15; excluding incumbents from the, 79–80; excluding internal candidates from the, 82–83; the positive and negative aspects of fit during, 19–20; the problem with unnecessary vs. necessary specialization, 9–10; support from institutional leadership during, 10–12; targeted efforts during, 17–19. *See also* Search committees

Family status: discrimination against, 7; inappropriate vs. permissible interview questions about, 106*t*

Federal-designated protected classes, 7

Fit: faculty searches and context of, 19–20; search committee agreement on what is meant by, 20

Florida A&M University, 17

Free time interview schedule, 85–87

**G**

Gender identity: discrimination against, 8; inappropriate vs. permissible interview questions about, 105*t*

George Washington University (GWU), 13–14

Goodman, D. F., 72

"Green card" requirements, 42–43

Gross, N., 4

*Guide to Best Practices in Faculty Search and Hiring* (Columbia University), 15–16

**H**

H visa hires: caution against mentioning salary in advertisements for, 39; permanent residency requirements in advertisements, 42–43

Hamilton College, 5

Hampton University, 17

Harvard University, 51

Health conditions: California's protected class of AIDS/HIV status, 8; discrimination against, 7; inappropriate vs. permissible interview questions about, 109*t*

Hewitt, G. J., 5

Higher education: *Brown v. Board of Education* impact on, 2; perceived as opportunities for social change, 2–3; protected classes in context of, 7–8, 18, 102–110*t*; "separate but equal" doctrine of, 2

Hiring. *See* Faculty searches

Hispanic (or Latino) faculty: cultural taxation phenomenon experienced by, 13;

diversity goal to increase representation of, 2–3; search committee membership of, 12–13

Hispanics (or Latinos): lack of faculty representation of, 2–3; US population percentage of, 2

Historically Black colleges and universities (HBCUs): Black faculty of, 2; targeting faculty applicants from, 17

Hochel, S., 76

Hosoda, M., 72

Howard University, 17

Hunter, J. E., 72

Hurtado, S., 4

Hypothetical interview questions, 94–96

**I**

"Illegal" interview questions. *See* Inadvisable interview questions

Illness status: California's protected class of AIDS/HIV status, 8; federal law prohibiting discrimination against, 7; inappropriate vs. permissible interview questions about, 109*t*

Inadvisable interview questions: birthday question thought experiment on, 102–104; description of, 102; protected classes and inappropriate or, 104, 105*t*–110*t*; what to do if one has been asked, 111–112

Incumbents: description of, 78–79; excluded from the search process, 79–80

*Indoctrinate U* (Maloney film), 3

Institutions: Historically Black colleges and universities (HBCUs), 2, 17; nondiscrimination statement of, 8; private, 8; reasons for considering matters of diversity in, 2–3; search advertisement information on, 41–42; targeting faculty searches to other, 17–18, 19; traditional lack of diversity in, 1–2; women's colleges, 17. *See also* Academic programs; Administration

Internal candidates: excluded from the search process, 82–83; interview before external candidates, 81; matching their experience to the other candidates, 82; never extend a courtesy interview to, 81; realtor involvement in interview of, 84–85; special procedures involving, 80–83

Internet-based search advertisements: impact of, 23; overview of different venues including, 29–35

Interpersonal relationships, 54

Physical challenges: discrimination against, 7; inappropriate vs. permissible interview questions about, 108*t*

Political ideologies: inappropriate vs. permissible interview questions about, 110*t*; pursuit of faculty with diverse, 4–5

Pregnancy status: federal law prohibiting discrimination against, 7; inappropriate vs. permissible interview questions about family or, 106*t*

Priority application deadlines, 45–46

Private institution "protected classes" exemptions, 8

Professional organizations' minority caucuses, 18

Protected classes: determining precise composition of institution's, 104; exemptions related to, 8; faculty search targeting conferences designed for, 18; federal-designated, 7; inadvisable birthday question thought experiment on, 102–104; inadvisable or inappropriate interview questions and, 104, 105*t*–110*t*; institution's nondiscrimination statement application to, 8; state-designated, 8

Pryor, J. H., 4

**Q**

Question-and-answer interviews: avoid questions that have clear right or wrong answers, 99; conclusion of the, 112; creative reframing of the common, 96–99; formal questions vs. during informal social situations, 111; "illegal" or inadvisable questions to ask, 102–112; including performance-based elements in, 93–94; open-ended preferred for, 98; posing hypothetical questions, 94–96; sample questions to use for effective, 92–93; scheduling the session, 77; steer clear of trite or stock, 98; as traditional interview approach, 92; yes-or-no questions during, 98, 99–100

**R**

Race: discrimination against, 7; inappropriate vs. permissible interview questions about, 107*t*

Realtors: candidate interview role of community, 83–85; pay attention to what they say about candidate's behavior, 84

Reference calls: best practices for making, 62–64; specific things to ask about candidates during, 65; two different times to make, 62–63

Religious status: discrimination against, 7; inappropriate vs. permissible interview questions about, 108*t*

**S**

Salary range information, 38–39

San Jose State University's "Academic Finalist Interview Evaluation Form," 51

Schmidt, F. L., 72

Screening applications: distinguishing qualified from unqualified applicants, 52–53; recommendations for search committee chairs on, 50–51

Search advertisement FAQs: on handling contract status, 37–38; on information on the institution, 41–42; on issue of rank, 37; on level of experience, 41; on permanent residency requirements, 42–43; on preferred or required degree, 39–40; on salary range, 38–39; on starting date, 40

Search advertisement process: step 1: decide on the most important information, 24–28; step 2: decide on most appropriate venues, 29–31; step 3: tailor the information to the specific venue, 31–32; step 4: track success rates of each venue and format, 33–35; step 5: adjust the strategy as needed, 35–36

Search advertisement tracking: A/B testing for, 33–35; online tools for, 34–35

Search advertisements: to advance and not hinder diversity goals, 16; application deadline information in, 46; "Don't bury the lead" in, 32; five-step process of posting, 23–36; frequently asked questions about, 36–43; include why faculty diversity is important in, 28; on the Internet, 23; phrasing of the, 14–16; problem with unnecessary specialization included in, 9–10; think about the position holistically for, 31

Search committee chairs: best practices to begin application process, 47–50; best practices when screening applications, 50–53; importance of clear guidance by the, 69–70

Search committees: best practices in conducting phone or video interviews, 65–67; best practices in reducing the short list of applicants, 58–62; best practices for